Embracing Risk in Urban Education

Curiosity, Creativity, and Courage in the Era of "No Excuses" and Relay Race Reform

Alice E. Ginsberg

ROWMAN & LITTLEFIELD EDUCATION
A division of
ROWMAN & LITTLEFIELD PUBLISHERS, INC.
Lanham • New York • Toronto • Plymouth, UK

Published by Rowman & Littlefield Education
A division of Rowman & Littlefield Publishers, Inc.
A wholly owned subsidary of The Rowman & Littlefield Publishing Group, Inc.
4501 Forbes Boulevard, Suite 200, Lanham, Maryland 20706
http://www.rowmaneducation.com

Estover Road, Plymouth PL6 7PY, United Kingdom

British Library Cataloguing in Publication Information Available

Library of Congress Cataloging-in-Publication Data

Ginsberg, Alice E.
Embracing risk in urban education : curiosity, creativity, and courage in the Era of "no excuses" and
relay race reform / Alice E. Ginsberg.
p. cm.
Includes bibliographical references and index.
Summary: "Ginsberg argues that in the effort to reduce the achievement gap and mitigate the pejorative label of "at-risk," we are in danger of eliminating risk from education entirely. This is especially
the case in urban schools with large numbers of poor and minority students. Ginsberg explores
alternative approaches to student achievement at four dynamic Philadelphia public schools"-- Provided by publisher.
ISBN 978-1-60709-948-2 (hardback) -- ISBN 978-1-60709-949-9 (paper) -- ISBN 978-1-60709-950-
5 (electronic)
1. Children with social disabilities--Pennsylvania--Philadelphia--Case studies. 2. Education, Urban--
Pennsylvania--Philadelphia--Case studies. 3. School improvement programs--Pennsylvania--Phila-
delphia--Case studies. I. Title.
LC4093.P5.G56 2012
371.826'940974811--dc23
                                                                        2011046715

The paper used in this publication meets the minimum requirements of American National
Standard for Information Sciences Permanence of Paper for Printed Library Materials,
ANSI/NISO Z39.48-1992.

Printed in the United States of America

"At once the very existence of obstacles depends on the desire to reach towards wider spheres of fulfillment, to expand options, to know alternatives. As has been said, a rock is an obstacle only to one who wants to climb the hill." —Maxine Greene, Dialectic of Freedom (1988)

Contents

Foreword

Untapped Possibilities

Upon invitation, Dr. Maxine Greene—a pioneer of progressive education— generously agreed to write the foreword for this book. Intrigued by the idea of "embracing risk" in urban education, the following is her personal reflection on what that entails, and why it must be a critical part of school reform in the twenty-first century.

To embrace risk is to open spaces in experience for the play of wonder and imagination. It involves a willingness to face the unpredictable and, at once, working to identify a range of untapped possibilities. "To look at things as if they could be otherwise" is one of John Dewey's concepts with regard to imagination and, even as that opens windows in experience, it reveals landscapes still unexplored, landscapes waiting to be cultivated by those with the courage and energy to act.

To take a risk is to open multiple unexplored spaces. It may involve entering a shared domain in process of becoming like the emergent spaces of the kind of "spring" taking shape in countries around the world. To take a risk is to refuse interference with personal growth or the efforts to transform new spaces in and around the world. Attending with optimism to the stirring of resistance to authority, we may find ourselves suddenly moving from hope in the face of a realization of possibility actualized to a kind of despair at the rise of restiveness and conflict among those choosing personal freedom while participating in developing democracy.

It is distressing to read of people adopting the messages in manifestos, like those of the "Unabomber." Generalizations about liberation from the thralls of capitalism and even from the slowness of idealistic reform have a tendency to freeze rational thought. We need to reflect on the vibrant moments of the 60s and 70s and on the disillusionment that followed in so many places, and to ponder how to respond.

We need to be willing to become wide awake, to see with open eyes. To allow for risk in the learning process is to draw attention to what is unknown to the learner, to what might be and what indeed should be. To refuse to take risks is to submit to complacency and the taken for granted. What is needed is a transformative approach to thinking and learning, a rejection of what has long been taken for granted.

Maxine Green, PhD

Dr. Maxine Greene is one of the primary influences on progressive education in the twentieth and twenty-first centuries. Author of more than ten books, Greene is a Professor at Teachers College and the Founder of the Maxine Greene Foundation for Social Imagination, the Arts and Education. She is past president of the American Educational Research Association and recipient of its Lifetime Achievement Award.

Acknowledgments

I would like to begin by thanking the founders, principals, teachers, students, and community partners of the four schools profiled in this book: the Science Leadership Academy, the Folk Arts Cultural Treasures School, Parkway NW School for Peace and Social Justice, and the Wissahickon Charter School. The schools were all most welcoming to me, giving me significant access to both daily classes and special events. I found that everyone involved was most generous with their time, eager to talk honestly with me about the risks and rewards they experienced as they attempted to create and reimagine the very conception of urban education.

It is easy to get cynical in these times that urban public education is all but "doomed." These schools proved to me over and over that the possibilities for creative success are limitless, and for this I am most grateful. I got to witness the beauty of youth who were fully engaged, curious, excited, pushing boundaries, surprising themselves and each other, critically questioning, courageously experimenting, and genuinely collaborating. I have no doubt they will be instrumental in the quest for social justice—indeed, they already are.

I would like to thank the visionary educators who contributed original quotes about *embracing risk in urban education*, and those who read various drafts of this book and provided invaluable feedback. For their ongoing support and encouragement I would especially like to thank my colleagues: Joan Shapiro, Shirley Brown, Marybeth Gasman, Donna Johnson, Audrey Cohen, and Andrea Honigsfeld.

I want to thank my publisher, Tom Koerner, vice president of the Education Division at Rowman & Littlefield, for his strong commitment to this book, as well as his obvious belief in supporting public education, progressive education, and educational equity. I believe that under his leadership Rowman & Littlefield is publishing some of the most exciting books in the field.

I very much want to thank Jon Wallace, who helped me turn hundreds of pages of research into a book. Frankly, he is one of the most talented editors I have ever met.

I thank Katherine Miller for her wisdom and support.

As always, I want to thank my friends and family. Watching my sons, Andrew and Nicholas Chalfen, as they moved from preschool to middle and high school, has always given me reason to think critically and creatively about education. I thank them for sharing so much of their journey with me, even when they knew it was going to (sigh) end up in print. To my husband, Samuel Chalfen, I can only say that your love, support, and belief in me are behind every word in this book.

Preface

When RISK Is a Four-Letter Word

"I promise to do each step in order and not try anything unknown."

The passage above was taken from a science contract that fourth-grade students *and* their parents were required to sign at the beginning of the school year. Although the school clearly wanted to ensure the students' safety, the choice of language here is not insignificant. The metaphorical interpretation of this single clause is at the center of understanding this book. Indeed, the day my own child came home with this very contract and asked me to cosign it was the day this book was conceived.

To be honest, I could *almost* stomach the first part of this clause: "I promise to do each step in order." The idea that education is a kind of race where all children must be kept "on track," running step by step in the same direction, at the same speed, at the same time, toward the same endpoint had ceased to be a far-right, highly conservative position. Even an African American, liberal, Democratic president who ran on the promise of hope and unity has become fixated on the idea of "winning" in education. According to President Obama: "To win the future . . . we also need to win the race to educate our kids . . . We need to out-innovate, out-educate, and out-build the rest of the world."[1]

President Obama's rhetoric about education, repeated constantly by his secretary of education, Arne Duncan, implies that knowledge is a scarce and fixed commodity that we must tightly hold onto or risk losing altogether. In any case, the idea is that there isn't enough knowledge to go around for everyone; if other countries excel in education, it can only mean that America is somehow losing, and vice versa. In place of the (seemingly) equitable

1

goals of No Child Left Behind, it might well be argued that America's current educational policy is more like No (American) Child Left Behind, or perhaps Every Other Country Left Behind.

I don't agree with this philosophy, but I do understand it. It comes from a place of genuine fear. It is the fear that certain groups of children—primarily those in poor, urban school districts with high concentrations of minority students—are dragging the predominance of the rest of the country down with low test scores and high dropout rates. (Thus, we become an entire nation at risk.) It is the fear that (certain groups of) Americans have long enjoyed economic and other privileges that we don't want to have to share with or "redistribute" to other countries. In short, it is the fear that if other countries progress, innovate, or transform, they may get to "the top" before we do. Once there, they may even push us out of reach. In any case, it is assumed that there is only so much room at "the top."

Those familiar with my previous books and articles know that I have always been an advocate of progressive education, and a staunch critic of the competitive, high-stakes testing ideology that is the bedrock of school-reform policies such as No Child Left Behind and now Race to the Top. Under the weight of these powerful mandates—which I have come to call Relay Race Reform—public schools have been becoming more rigid, more scripted, and more "bottom-line" oriented. (The bottom line here is something called "adequate yearly progress" and 100 percent "proficiency," both of which are based on standardized tests in but two subjects: math and reading.)

Despite years of compelling critiques of the reliability and validity of such tests, as well as countless testimonies from teachers themselves as to the dangerous impact of narrowing the curriculum with the sole purpose of preparing students to take these tests, the belief that these tests are our best measure of student achievement, and of our public-school system more generally, continues to gain strength. In fact, test scores are now being touted as the key to *all* aspects of measuring and "fixing" public schools, including proposals to tie test results to school funding, management and choice, teacher compensation and tenure, and student promotion. It is clear that Relay Race Reform is not going away any time soon. Instead we are raising the stakes.

But seriously:

"I promise not to try anything unknown." (??????)

Surely there had to be another way for the school to state this. Isn't the whole premise of education to *venture into the unknown*? Isn't that the definition of genuine *learning*: experiencing and/or understanding something new? Even in the current educational climate, where the result of learning is increasingly being reduced to a series of narrowly defined truths and right answers, asking students to *literally sign away* their right to explore the unknown has got to be seen as problematic. Are we really ready to ask students (and parents) to sign a contract promising *not* to be curious, *not* to test assumptions, *not* to be creative and open-minded, *not* to experiment, *not* to surprise themselves, *not* to see things from a new perspective, and *not* to seek alternative answers and solutions?

It is the premise of this book that in the effort to take the risk out of what is increasingly being thought of as an entire "nation at risk," we are in danger of taking the practice and value of "risk" out of education entirely. The concern at the center of this book is that, in this climate of school reform, it is becoming rarer and rarer for schools to be safe places for students to experiment, disagree, challenge authority, assert their individuality, test assumptions, and question data. I fear that, in an effort to "close the achievement gap" and maintain (or regain) American economic superiority, *risk* in public education has become something of a four-letter word.

Schools no longer focus on teaching and modeling the tenets of democracy (free speech, tolerance, diversity, public service, collaboration, and equal representation) for the next generation of leaders. Instead American public schools are increasingly embracing a "no excuses" business model of operation that focuses on strict competition, order and efficiency, static power hierarchies where teachers teach until students "get it," and punishing (or what many have called "pushing out") students who aren't performing as expected. When there are "no excuses" for failure, there are likely "no second chances" either.

Ironically, not too long after my son came home with the science contract in hand, I came across a comic in my local newspaper that pretty well summed up my concerns:

TEXT:

Father: So how was school today?

Daughter: Pretty cool actually! We learned about something called "The Bill of Rights."

F: Great! What've you learned so far?

D: That they're vague enough for agenda twisting, so there's a need for me to write some new ones!

F: (pausing, sighing heavily) I keep forgetting about the dark side of education.[2]

I wrote this book in hopes of shedding light on what is increasingly being dubbed "the dark side" of education. As a nation in fear of being "out-educated," we've become much too comfortable with the idea that there is simply no time or place for students to critically question, add to, or "re-write" standardized knowledge. America's job is to *broker it*, plain and simple. In a climate of *Relay Race Reform*, Freire's now classic description of the "banking model" of education—where a teacher's job is to *transfer* or *deposit* knowledge into students' brains—is perhaps more relevant than ever.

At the same time, I continue to read compelling accounts of schools that not only make space for children to explore the unknown but have, in fact, been created for that very purpose. I found four of these schools in my own backyard: the Science Leadership Academy, the Folk Arts Cultural Treasures School, the Parkway Northwest School for Peace and Social Justice, and the Wissahickon Charter School. Months of observations and interviews convinced me that these were indeed extraordinary examples of schools that nurture children's curiosity, creativity, and courage. In short, these are schools that exemplify what I call *embracing risk* in education.

Though they are all urban public schools within the School District of Philadelphia, I was drawn to this particular combination of schools because they have such different histories, student bodies, physical locations, and thematic focuses. Reading their stories collectively underscores my belief that there is no one best model for public education, that the possibilities for creative and innovative pedagogy and curricula are nearly endless. Whether it be through creating months-long folk arts residencies for minority and immigrant children, taking city kids to a farm in Vermont for a week to milk cows and make their own cheese, partnering with a local science museum to give students an opportunity to help design and curate exhibits, or sponsoring student-run "mediation" workshops and teach-ins on gender, racism, and violence for their peers, there is much to be learned here.

I wrote this book primarily to offer proof, hope, and inspiration to educators—especially teachers and aspiring teachers—that even in the scripted, narrow, and highly punitive context of No Child Left Behind and Race to the Top, there are still alternatives. Perhaps more importantly, I wrote this book to document the many ways that education can be much more meaningful and enriching to students who are able to take risks, which ultimately serves our entire society better as well. Though I realize that many of the examples in this book would be difficult (if not impossible) to implement many in American schools, I hope to at least start a conversation and complicate the debate about whether closing the achievement gap for at-risk children is best served by eliminating "risk" altogether.

While writing this book, I reached out to other educators across the United States, asking them for their own definitions of *embracing risk* in urban education. The appendix includes original statements from Maxine Greene,

Jacqueline Ancess, Peter McLaren, Wayne Au, Kathy Shultz, Christopher Robbins, Fredrick Erickson, and many others. One such statement, emailed to me by Margaret Smith Crocco, dean of the College of Education at the University of Iowa, seems particularly apt here:

> Risk, risk-taking, at-risk: how different the valence is for each of these terms. We calculate risk algorithms; we valorize certain forms of risk-taking; we joke about the possible pleasures associated with "risky business." . . . Schools need to be places where all the nation's children, whatever their backgrounds, are encouraged to take intellectual risks that move them (and sometimes us) outside our comfort zones. Dealing with the complex cognitive demands of the twenty-first century will require tolerance of ambiguity, respect for diversity, and appreciation of the benefits of risk-taking. Much is "at-risk" in the future of education. Are we up to the challenge?

Crocco asks: "Are we up to the challenge?" This is a very good question, and it is not a rhetorical one. Many believe that what Crocco calls "tolerance of ambiguity" and "respect for diversity" will further harm an already dying system. They believe that the best solution for American public education is complete standardization, a condensed focus and a more targeted end-game, and a return to the pedagogy of lecture and direct instruction—all of which further reduce learning to the resulting test scores.

Others believe the opposite: that the answer to problems in public education is to get rid of it altogether. They believe that public education fails because it is essentially a monopoly without accountability or genuine competition. The full privatization of public education is something we must all be prepared for, but creating greater "competition" is in no way the same thing as what Crocco calls "tolerating ambiguity." Eliminating free public education will not increase innovation and respect for diversity as much as it will make it easier for big companies to profit from it. Where business is concerned, ambiguity and diversity are only as useful as they are, eventually, salable.

As we explore together an entirely different path—*embracing* rather than *erasing* risk—I hope that at the end of this book readers will find themselves, as Crocco suggests, taking intellectual risks and pushing outside their comfort zones. I hope that even teachers who work in the most traditional school settings will find the opportunity, voice, and courage to challenge "the dark side" of education, even if it begins with a single, unexpected or prickly question. As educational reformer Sam Chaltain suggests in *American Schools,* we need to openly identify and address what we have "informally agreed never to talk about."[3] (With apologies to my son's science teacher) I ask you to join me as we collectively promise to step out of order, and to try something unknown.

NOTES

1. Barack Obama, State of the Union Address, January 25, 2011.
    2. From *"Non Sequitur"*, Philadelphia Inquirer, January 31, 2011.
    3. Sam Chaltain, *American Schools: The Art of Creating a Democratic Learning Community* (Lanham, MD: Rowman & Littlefield, 2010), 61.

Introduction

Why Embrace *Risk in Education?*

Here's what some prominent educators, policymakers, journalists, and philanthropists have had to say recently about American public education:

> The truth is, the state of American education is pitiful, and it's getting worse.
> —Michele Rhee, former superintendent of D.C. schools and founder of *Students First*[1]

> The bad news is that for years now we've been getting out-educated. . . . Have no illusions. We're in a hole.
> —Thomas L. Friedman, *New York Times* columnist[2]

> We've taken on some tough issues: eradicating malaria . . . combating family homelessness. Out of everything our foundation does, improving education in America may be the toughest challenge we've taken on.
> —Bill and Melinda Gates, cofounders of Microsoft Corp. and leading educational philanthropists[3]

> Fifty years later, our generation's Sputnik moment is back. . . . As it stands right now America is in danger of falling behind.
> —President Barack Obama [4]

> It is difficult to dislodge the educational establishment. In New Orleans, a hurricane was required: since Katrina, New Orleans has made more educational progress than any other city, largely because the public-school system was wiped out.
> —Education reporters Evan Thomas and Pat Wingert[5]

> The traditional public-school system is what ultimately needs to be changed
> for us to change the horrific status quo we have been living with in America.
> —Geoffrey Canada, charter school leader[6]

Any way you look at it, the first decade of the twenty-first century did not
end well for American public education. In 2010 it was almost impossible to
open a magazine or newspaper, watch the nightly news or television talk
shows, listen to the radio, or even go to the movie theater without being
bombarded by the brutal statistics of how our public schools are failing—and
failing *miserably*. In fact, some consider our public schools to be such a
disaster that a hurricane wiping them out entirely is actually hailed as a
blessing in disguise.

Over the course of writing this book—now well into 2011—things are not
looking up for public education. If anything, the need to completely reform
public education has become even more "urgent." Former New York City
schools chancellor Joel Klein recently said, "While American students are
stuck in a ditch, the rest of the world is moving ahead. . . . Time is running
out." [7]

Is time is running out?

At present, it is predicted that 82 percent of American schools will fail to
meet adequate yearly standards (as mandated by No Child Left Behind) this
year, not to mention fall far short of the goal of 100 percent student proficiency by 2014. By the last official count, the United States ranked fourteenth out
of thirty-four OECD[8] countries for reading skills, seventeenth for science,
and twenty-fifth for mathematics. While many claimed to be "stunned" by
this news, Secretary of Education Arne Duncan warned, "We have to see this
as a wake-up call. . . . We can quibble or face the brutal truth that we are
being out-educated."[9]

In this climate of widespread failure, and at what Duncan calls a time of
"extraordinary risk,"[10] I realize that the title of this book is both provocative
and somewhat puzzling. *Embracing* risk? *Haven't we already risked too
much?* Indeed, haven't we identified ourselves as an entire nation at risk, in
imminent danger of being outsmarted and economically marginalized by
other countries? Isn't our public-education system characterized by an increasing number of mediocre schools overflowing with students who are
reading and writing below grade level, unable to do basic math, dropping out
at unprecedented numbers, ill-prepared go to college, and in danger of becoming teenage parents, welfare recipients, or following the school-to-prison
pipeline?

Although criticism of our public-school system is not exactly new, over
the last decade discussions about public-school reform have become increasingly driven by a rhetoric of fear and panic, competition and consumerism,
rather than equity and democracy. As the quotes at the beginning of this

Introduction suggest, the language of public-school reform is riddled with words and phrases like *flat-lining, out-educated, in a hole, horrific,* and *pitiful.* Moreover, these terms are preceded by grim warnings such as *have no illusions, the truth is, the bad news is,* and *America is in danger.* (And in case you are not panicked enough by now, remember that the situation is only *getting worse.*)

The message about American public schools in the twenty-first century is stern and clear: something drastic has to be done. We must act quickly and decisively. In other words: there can be no more "excuses" for failure. We can have *zero tolerance* for deviancy. Our present mission, as far as education is concerned, has been clearly defined by the current administration: we are in a "Race to the Top." Secretary of Education Duncan has bluntly stated: "The educational reform movement is not a table where we all sit around and talk. It's a train that is leaving the station."[11] Former New York City Schools chancellor Joel Klein likewise argues that calls for "collaboration" in education reform are simply "bad advice." According to Klein: "Collaboration is the elixir of the status quo crowd."[12]

In place of talking and collaborating, we are moving to a strategy best exemplified by the reform movement catchphrase "whatever it takes."[13] We will do *whatever it takes* to ensure that our students test the highest in the world, and bring financial wealth and predominance back to America. Less and less is said about the role of education in sustaining American democracy, as well as in building a more just, connected global community where we reach across national identities to support and help each other.

Indeed, as America has struggled economically and become more competitive with other countries for jobs and resources, the ways in which we envision the value of public schools, the production of knowledge, and the education of youth have become increasingly nationalistic, xenophobic, and militaristic. One need only to look to the poster advertising the 2010 hit documentary *Waiting for Superman* to get a good picture of what guides most school reform in this century. It is the rhetoric of *fear* accompanied by the threat of *destruction.*

Picture: *A young white girl with blond hair is seen smiling, sitting upright at her desk, her textbook open as she obediently raises her hand. In the background, she is surrounded by an utter wasteland, depicted mostly in shades of grey. There are no other students, no teachers or adults of any kind. The all-important blackboard lies on the ground by her feet, covered in senseless scribbles.* The headline reads: "The fate of our country won't be decided on a battlefield, it will be determined in a classroom."[14]

What's at risk here? Nothing less than America's national security, our freedom, our prosperity, our very right to exist. If we buy into this vision, it is fair to ask why we should even *tolerate* risk in education, much less *embrace* it?

Yet, as I will argue here, there are different ways of defining and looking at the concept of risk in education. One is from an inherently deficit perspective that carries with it the fear of eminent danger and destruction. This is linked to the idea that we must tightly control everything that goes on in schools and place the maintenance of order, discipline, time on-task, and pure content coverage over any kind of critical thinking, disagreement, difficult dialogues, or creative and courageous action. What this means in policy and practice is:

- Increased efforts toward regulating, standardizing, scripting, and quantifying all knowledge and curricula taught in American public schools;
- Creating a school climate akin to a business marketplace (one that thrives on individual competition and profit), based on strictly enforced rules regarding authority, efficiency, and regulation; and
- Relying on narrowly focused standardized testing (currently in but two subjects, math and reading) as the primary means to evaluate student achievement, teacher competency, and sometimes the fate of entire schools and school districts.

This construction of education not only trivializes the majority of subjects taught in schools but also marginalizes other important school functions, such as teaching children the skills and concepts related to national and global citizenship, social justice, patience, empathy, sustained commitment, community and coalition building, and cooperative, responsive leadership.

It also suggests that students themselves bring little to the table; their job is to absorb information, not to question it. Their job is to sequentially recall information in narrowly defined contexts, not recreate it or "extract knowledge from information."[15] In other words, the sheer quantity of information retained trumps what students are able to *do* with that information in different contexts and for different purposes. As many progressive educators and activists have long warned, the process of learning has become decontextualized from the process of doing; knowledge is presented to students as something preordained, stagnant and uncontestable, rather than constructed, dynamic, and contestable.

A growing body of school-reform research and literature, for example, praises "no excuses" schools in which children are compelled to be organized, unified, respectful, on-task, and orderly. It says little about the darker side of these same virtues, which could be read as obedient, submissive, conforming, and unquestioning. Many such schools are being praised for rewarding students who "follow the rules" with material goods and increased resources. And these same schools are being praised for punishing students who rebel in any way by publically shaming them in front of their peers (e.g., by forcing them to wear an inside-out T-shirt or sit on a bench, or by forbidding them to talk).

There is also significant evidence to suggest that teachers at many public schools are increasingly encouraged to sort students according to their *perceived* level of risk and to tailor or differentiate their teaching accordingly. While there is nothing wrong with acknowledging multiple intelligences and learning styles, the goal here is something quite different and very specific in nature: *it is to reduce the risk that students will not perform well on standardized tests.*

Indeed, it is not uncommon in this age of high-stakes testing for teachers to be asked to assess their children in terms of the potential risk that they will bring down the collective scores of a classroom, school, or district. Some educators have gone as far as to refer to "bubble children," separating out the "slippables" and "pushables."[16] The paradoxical result is that instead of erasing inequalities, teachers end up using pedagogical practices that further stigmatize and reproduce these divisions. As Christopher Robbins has noted, the consequence of using test scores to evaluate success and failure is that "students already placed at risk are seen as risks to teacher competency evaluations and school funding."[17]

The very category or label "at-risk," then, must be scrutinized, even as we all (theoretically) agree that it is vitally important to close the achievement gap. It is the premise of this book that the stories behind the statistics that render entire cultures "at-risk" are powerful stories not simply of low expectations, uncaring teachers and parents, cultural deprivation, individual laziness, and low intelligence *but instead of political capital, misused power, and unjustly distributed resources.*

They are also stories denoting ways that culturally dominant values and expectations interact (or in some cases *collide*) with entrenched systems of inequality that pervade our entire nation—health care, social welfare, housing, criminal justice, employment—systems too often studied in isolation from one another.

Moreover, as many have pointed out before me, the "at-risk" label seems to focus entirely on what *might* happen, and, more specifically, on what *bad things* might happen to children identified with certain cultural groups and socioeconomic communities. The label "at-risk" has become synonymous with a *deficit* model of difference, leading those with more power, wisdom and expertise to try to "save" these children from themselves and, ironically, from their own cultures, voices, and communities.

Indeed, many students considered most "at-risk" are those who most blatantly challenge dominant values and accepted "truths" about American history and culture, including what makes America "great" and the extent to which we have practiced and realized our democratic ideals of individual freedom and equal opportunity. Students who challenge cultural stereotypes and refute simplistic depictions of minorities in textbooks, worksheets, and standardized tests are often our most engaged students. And yet, they are also likely to be seen as "troublemakers" in a system that is more concerned with efficiency and orderliness than with critical pedagogy.

There has been little recognition that children from so-called "at-risk" communities also bring significant experiences, insight, knowledge, imagination, curiosity, wisdom, cultural treasures, and other strengths with them to school. Not the least of these has been the creativity, resilience, and courage to actively resist practices that further marginalize, silence, or degrade them.

While the increased emphasis on multicultural education that began in the 1980s and 1990s has been a step in the right direction, multiculturalism has been impeded by its failure to incorporate the concept of *intersectionality* or intersecting oppressions. Intersectionality underscores how cultural identities and labels ("us" vs. "them") are always constructed in connection with and comparison to other groups. Cultural identity thus shifts in different contexts, and is contested and reified from different standpoints and hierarchies of power. Too often, multiculturalism becomes about equal representation rather than deconstructing the values, systems, and actions that define *equal* and *representation*.

The concept of cultural identity is not, in other words, as unitary and homogeneous as we tend present it in schools, even when we are trying to teach respect for it. When schools try to become more multicultural and to serve heterogeneous student populations, they often end up simply reifying cultural and binary stereotypes and categories as schools still cling to "add-and-stir" or "melting pot" pedagogies. Put another way, under the guise of "respect" for different cultures, many multicultural programs have sought to teach individuals from culturally oppressed groups to embrace the "codes of power," rather than encourage them to collectively deconstruct them, challenge them and act with courage and intent to change them.[18]

Why? Because it can be very "risky" to highlight cultural conflicts and inequities when many of these conflicts still *actively impact* the lives of students every day. Moreover, collective action can be tricky because it means that students must begin to explore how their own thoughts and actions may be complicit in someone else's inequality or subordination. As Patricia Hill-Collins has rightly noted, the very concept of oppression is filled with contradictions as there are few pure victims or oppressors.[19]

In place of the (often unstated but highly entrenched) goal of cultural assimilation and order, this book presents an argument for creating public schools where youth can openly explore the politics of difference, and actively challenge the structures and practices of inequity, oppression, and marginalization. These schools would be places where students would have a wide variety of opportunities, within the core curriculum and as an explicit part of the educational mission of the school, to critically reflect on and experiment with their own roles in the struggle for change and social justice.

Moreover, these would be schools where youth are motivated by far more than carrots and sticks: good grades, the opportunity to earn extra privileges (such as longer recess or vouchers to spend at the school store), or the fear of getting in trouble and/or being publically shamed. Not only would students be motivated by genuine curiosity and desire to learn, but they would be assured of a genuine voice and investment in the school community. School, in other words, would not be something "done to" students or an obstacle course they have to wade through in order to reach their "real lives." School-work would be both relevant and meaningful to the lives students are living now, as well as to the futures they are helping to create and will be an integral part of.

The view of risk that I embrace in this book, then, is one in which teaching and learning is a messy and inherently *unfinished* process that depends on being able to use knowledge obtained in one context when the context changes—as it most certainly will. When learning becomes solely about memorization and recall, it stymies students' motivation, along with their belief that they can be active and effective agents of change. As Patrick Finn has rightly noted: "If we teach children to critique without teaching them to act, we instill cynicism and despair."[20]

The title of this book, *Embracing Risk in Urban Education*, is thus meant to challenge the ideology that risk is inherently negative. Risk is both the means by and the channel through which we experiment with change, innovate, and look for better strategies and solutions. As educator Nathalia Jaraqmillo says, "I would argue that taking risks is constitutive of the learning process. Without risks, we find ourselves at a stalemate."[21] Put another way, without risk we cannot help but reify the *status quo*.

Seen in this context, what we are really risking when we allow risk to remain part of education is not *failure* but *change*. When we work collaboratively, we risk having our minds changed. When we are asked to use knowledge to engage in and help solve real-world problems, we risk social and political upheaval. When we allow for resistance and transgression, we must also be prepared for transformation. When we open the door for so-called "excuses" and "second chances," we refuse to simply write off or silence children who disagree with us.

Embracing risk means that students are constantly asking their own questions and reflecting on what they are doing in school with the understanding that knowledge goes beyond memorization of basic skills. Schools must cultivate a space where students can question how and why certain knowledge is validated, marginalized and/or completely dismissed. In other words, knowledge does not in itself equal power. It's not just *what* we know; it's *how* we know it, *why* we believe it to be true/relevant, and how we are prepared to *use it* in practice.

Likewise, schools must be places where students feel safe enough to ask critical and often uncomfortable questions about the historic discrimination against and domination of certain racial and cultural groups within larger social structures and systems of power. Deborah Meier underscores when we are faced with irreconcilable ideas we are challenged to learn to invent new ones. Similarly, Jacqueline Ancess asks, "Do we want our schools to lecture students about the values and principles of our democracy or operationalize them so they can find meaning in them?"[22]

More bluntly, *embracing risk* in education means that we may be faced with the possibility that American youth will challenge and possibly be complicit in the redistribution of long-entrenched systems of wealth, power, and privilege—a goal that, obviously, not all stakeholder groups support. As Kohn sarcastically suggests in *When 21st-Century Schooling Just Isn't Good Enough: A Modest Proposal*, schools should "deliberately discourage real critical thinking on the part of students, since this may lead them to pose inconvenient questions about the entire enterprise and ideology on which it's based."[23]

In other words, do we continue to believe that education alone, as defined by the memorization of large amounts of facts and data, can be society's great equalizer? Or do we want to concede that that public schools, like all public institutions, do not exist within a vacuum, and traditional definitions of educational success will not always be enough to overcome inequities in other parts of American society?

For example, when we teach children that there are "no excuses" for failure (a growing educational ideology discussed in chapter 1), we are implying that substantial obstacles that perpetuate social inequality are, in actuality, trivial and can be pushed aside or ignored. As David Levin, founder of the growing KIPP Charter Schools, tells his students: "We want students, who, when we say, 'Run through that wall,' will run because they believe something is good on the other side."[24] However good his intentions, Levin does not say much about the serious repercussions of severe head trauma.

There is an important caveat here, however: I am not suggesting that we teach disadvantaged students to be cynical and feel hopeless. I am suggesting just the opposite. We must create spaces within all public institutions that foster public input, empowerment, and influence. Rather than having them run through a wall because an authority figure assures them that there is "something good" on the other side, we need to create opportunities for students to work collectively to systemically remap or dismantle these walls, ultimately opening a path for others to follow them with greater safety and success.

Anticipating the cries of "anarchy!" I must underscore here that *embracing risk* in education is not the same thing as *anything goes*. John Dewy said it best in *Democracy and Education*:

> Open-mindedness is not the same thing as empty-mindedness. To hand out a sign saying 'Come right in; there is no one at home,' is not the equivalent of hospitality."[25]

I intend to demonstrate how school-based organization and learning can be "risky" without being unstructured, unsupervised, or unnecessarily chaotic. As I will soon discuss in greater detail, the schools profiled here provide rich evidence that some of the riskiest schools are also the most thoughtful, reflective, and visionary. These are schools where the concept of "hospitality" stretches way beyond the classic school directive: "Take a seat."

I am also not suggesting that there are no consequences involved in *embracing risk*—in education or in any aspect of our lives. Obviously, risk can be both debilitating and liberating, often at the same time and for different groups of people. Some risks pay off, others don't. While I strongly believe that schools need to let students embrace risk, these risks must be accompanied by thorough and honest reflection: *Was the risk we took effective? Did it bring about the change we'd hoped for or envisioned? Who is taking the real risk, and who is most likely to benefit from it? Were there aspects of risk that we failed to consider?*

Perhaps most importantly, we need to reflect on our risks in preparation for moving forward: *Have we provided the necessary support systems to help us when risks backfire?* and *Is it likely that, despite our best efforts, we will face these same, or similar, risks again? If so, will we be prepared to reassess these risks and to reorganize our efforts appropriately?* In other words, as educator and activist Debbie Wei has urged, we must support risk without supporting the *glamorization* of risk. Inherent in the process of taking risks, then, is having the humility and adaptability to rethink our assumptions and our actions. We must encourage students to be critical thinkers and creative problem-solvers, while also considering that not all solutions will work equally well in all contexts and for all stakeholders.

Framed in this way, to embrace risk in education does not promote chaos and national insecurity, but rather is a prerequisite for strengthening and sustaining democracy. Risk, when accompanied by supportive structures and appropriate opportunities for reflection and empathy, is the part of education that students will likely remember the most. If we surprise ourselves, if we change our minds, we are not returning to the same place; we have created a new path. As Sam Chaltain writes: "Meaningful learning is risky, difficult, and sometimes painful. But it's also sometimes the moment when we first discover what we're capable of, and why we can never go back."[26]

CHOOSING SCHOOLS: A CASE STUDY APPROACH

In conceiving of this book, I wanted to do much more than write "theoretically" about the consequences of eliminating risk from public education or, alternatively, the value of embracing risk in urban education. I wanted to provide concrete examples of schools that are explicitly committed to this endeavor. I wanted to write a book that would consider how different schools define and assess risk in the current climate of educational policy and funding, while also looking closely at the day-to-day, grounded innovations in curriculum, pedagogy, and school structure have made this work possible and noteworthy.

The majority of this book (chapters 2 through 5) thus consists of profiles of four urban public schools that exemplify the practice of embracing risk, in both theory and in practice. In addition to looking closely at the founding principles, mission statements, core values, and standards that were carefully developed—indeed, communally crafted—at each of these schools, I give examples in pedagogy and curriculum of what educators and students are actually doing. These examples are culled from classroom and school wide observation, as well as from interviews with teachers, students, administrators, and other members of the school community.

As much as possible, I include teachers' own perspectives on why they approached a lesson plan in a particular way, what they think were the most salient aspects and teachable moments, and what they might do differently in the future and why. I also include student voices and provide examples from students' work, including the questions they ask along the way, the (often uncomfortable or previously silenced) issues that engaging in such work raises for them, and the ways in which they have played an important role in directing and reflecting upon their own learning process.

In many cases, I include (anonymous) excerpts from students' evaluations, written reflections, journals, and poems because I have found that these more creative and less restrained forms of expression can also be significantly more honest and thought-provoking than those culled from interviews or surveys. There are a number of reasons this might be true, including the most obvious: students anticipate what adults want to hear when they are questioned in relationships of unequal power.

While I provide varying levels of detail regarding the units of study, lesson plans, assignments, pedagogical approaches, and institutional practices that take place in these schools, in each case I try to underscore the ways in which *product* and *process* do not have to be dichotomized. In each of these schools, students are learning important and broad-based content knowledge about history, science, math, and literature, among other subjects. They are doing well on state standardized tests and, in the case of the high schools I profile, have impressive acceptance rates for college.

But the *ways* in which students are learning, experiencing, and using this content is not standard practice for public education. As much as possible, I underscore how and why these are more meaningful, useful, and sustained ways for students to learn, and I highlight how they *embrace risk* in a positive way. The examples chosen for this collection represent some of the most creative and forward-thinking pedagogy I have ever witnessed.

I hope that these detailed examples will not only inspire other educators to embrace risk, but also reassure them that straying from the traditional "banking model" or lecture format will not necessarily compromise student learning. In fact, I believe that these stories prove just the opposite.

That said, at the end of each chapter, I pose a series of questions designed to help readers visualize how these kinds of practices would (or would not) bring added quality or value to their own school/work, as well as the concrete steps they could take to support a school environment that *embraces risk.* I also raise critical questions that must accompany those risks—especially given the realities of what is possible in different socioeconomic, political, and bureaucratic structures.

Finally, as I discuss in greater detail through the chapters to follow, I chose schools that had very different histories, student bodies, founding principles, models of leadership, and relationships to the communities they are in. Importantly, I chose a combination of charter schools and district schools. While I marvel at what some charter schools have accomplished, this book is not intended in any way to argue that they are superior to the district model. In fact, the charter schools I profile in this book are unique one-of-a-kind schools that were conceived and built collaboratively over a period of years by concerned educators, activists, and/or parents from the very communities in which those schools now thrive.

In writing about these schools, I struggled with whether to keep each school as a discrete chapter/case study, given that they shared many common values and ideologies. In the end I decided that it was important to describe each school separately, and in as much detail as I could, to emphasize how different organizational, pedagogical, and curricular approaches, when aligned, can sustain, reinforce, challenge, and enrich one another. In other words, while I support small steps toward bringing students outside their comfort zones and exploring the unknown, it is important to see how one such experience supports and enables another.

I wanted to look at schools that were public and depended largely on public funding, and that had large populations of children of color, immigrant children, and children living in poverty. I thus chose schools that were all in an urban area, and titled this book *Embracing Risk in Urban Education.*

This is because I believe that children in urban schools are among those we are most quick to label (pejoratively) "at-risk." Urban schools are more often designated as persistently dangerous or failing, and even when they are not, they are often situated in communities with less material resources and bottom-up input into the reform process. As Pedro Noguera rightfully states:

> Increasingly, the term *urban* is less likely to be employed as a geographic concept used to define and describe physical locations than as a social or cultural construct used to describe certain people and places. . . . Changes in nomenclature reflect more than just ideological and political trends. The association between the term *urban* and people and places that are poor and non-White is tied to demographic and economic transformations that occurred in cities throughout the United Sates during the past 50 years.[27]

Urban schools are often at the center of debates about closing the "achievement gap," and thus have been the focus of much of my work. Having said that, I think all schools would benefit from the practices and ideas expressed herein.

CHAPTER OUTLINE

Chapter 1 of this book seeks to unpack the rhetoric of contemporary school reform by looking closely at the language we use to think and talk about educational practices and policy, and, specifically, where the concept of "risk" fits into these ideologies. I will use techniques associated with Critical Discourse Analysis (CDA), which draws out the connections between language and power. In other words, CDA requires a shift from seeing language as neutral expression of fact to the understanding that (intentionally or not) our choice of words reflects our particular historical, social, and political subjectivities. In this chapter I consider some of the explicit and implicit assumptions in the language of current debates around:

- "good" teaching and school leadership;
- fair and effective student assessment;
- school wide culture and discipline;
- student motivation and incentives to achieve;
- how to address and/or reform underperforming schools;
- how to close the achievement gap for "at-risk" and disadvantaged students;
- curricula and content standards; and
- diverse pedagogies of teaching and learning.

While the rhetoric and arguments that support these policies may *seem* to be about the virtues of meritocracy, personal responsibility, and individual hard work, there is also a strong component of separating, sorting, marginalizing, and punishing students—*and teachers and schools themselves*—who refuse to conform to the status quo.

Chapter 2 explores a public high school in the Philadelphia School District called the Science Leadership Academy (SLA), which was developed in close collaboration and partnership with Philadelphia's renowned science museum, the Franklin Institute (TFI). The SLA *embraces risk* by using the experimental, hands-on method of problem-solving and inquiry-based learning associated with the sciences *across the entire curriculum*. Moreover, the school seeks to use twenty-first-century technologies in all aspects of teaching and learning, not only to make learning more relevant and useful to students in a rapidly changing global context, but also to allow students to explore a wide range of self-expression, communication, cultural exchange, and intelligences.

Indeed, a large part of what makes the SLA noteworthy, and why it is featured in this book, is that in addition to more traditional tests, students are continually asked to "create" and publicly share something original, essentially making the end of learning yet another kind of beginning. Students at the SLA regularly create videos, podcasts, blogs and wikis, commercials and public service ads, political T-shirts, business plans, and policy recommendations, and they engage in playwriting, poetry, drama, dance, and expressive movement.

Chapter 3 explores a small community K–8 charter school called the Folk Arts Cultural Treasures School (FACTS), which was designed to serve as a positive alternative for minority and immigrant children whose cultures are often marginalized in traditional school contexts. Rather than using a *deficit* model of education—in which students need to be better assimilated into mainstream American culture—the FACTS *embraces risk* by helping students critique and deconstruct the very processes by which we create and reify culture.

In the process, the FACTS uses the concept of the *folk arts* as a guiding methodology to understand and emphasize the skills, knowledge, and meaningful exchanges that are central to living cultural traditions. Thus folk arts may include illustration, stories, songs, and dances, but they may also include sayings, proverbs, games, greetings, rituals, and memories. Calling such traditions "folk" is a way of underscoring the fact that communities are collectively built and thrive on shared ideas, visions, traditions, and the wisdom of their elders.

Chapter 4 centers on Parkway Northwest School for Peace and Social Justice, a high school created partially in response to the growth of public military academies in the school district, and the perceived need for balance in the form of a school that specifically addressed the detrimental and unnecessary violence defining the lives of so many students in the community. Parkway NW *embraces risk* by exploring alternatives to violence, and engaging students in mediation workshops, collaborative learning, and a pedagogy of real-world problem-solving, with an emphasis on both local and global issues.

In addition to creating a safe environment within the school for students to learn without fear, Parkway teaches students that they have both the power and the obligation to help others in need. The school offers opportunities for students to work together to fundamentally change the systems that create such desolation in the first place. Students at Parkway regularly take part in in-service learning and participate in policy discussions and research. This work is accompanied by opportunities to design and lead community protests and revitalization efforts, fundraising, peer mediation seminars, student "teach-ins," and diverse global exchanges on topics ranging from sexuality and gender roles to racial equity and immigration law.

Chapter 5 concludes the case studies with an exploration of the Wissahickon Charter School, a K–8 charter school with an environmental focus that teaches children about the interconnectedness of the physical and human (both urban and rural) environments. The school *embraces risk* through an interdisciplinary curriculum based on central challenges and analysis of real-world problems and policy issues such as those surrounding pollution, composting and recycling, the economics of transporting and selling food in different communities, and building sustainable cities locally and globally.

Bridging theory and action, students designed the school's playground; are responsible for maintaining a working school garden, recycling, and compost program; provide healthier lunch choices; and use a local park to expand its resources and curriculum. To supplement these more limited excursions into nature, the school offers regular class trips, from overnight cabin and tent camping, to backpacking and canoeing excursions, to full-week Outward Bound immersions.

In the book's conclusion, I look across the four schools to summarize some of the common characteristics, defining values, and pedagogical approaches that, together, exemplify the concept of *embracing risk* in education. This summary is expanded by the appendix, in which educators from across the country define, in their own words, what it means to *embrace risk* in urban education.

NOTES

1. Michelle Rhee, "What I've Learned," *Newsweek*, December 13, 2010, 40.

2. Thomas Friedman, *New York Times*, November 21, 2010.

3. Bill and Melinda Gates, "Educating Young People for the Global Economy," in *Waiting for Superman: How We Can Save America's Schools* K. Weber (New York: Public Affairs, 2010), 203.

4. Barack Obama, State of the Union Address, January 25, 2011.

5. Thomas Evans and Patrick Wingert, Newsweek, March 2010.

6. Geoffrey Canada, "Bringing Change to Scale," in *Waiting for Superman*, 192.

7. Joel Klein, "Scenes from the Class Struggle," *The Atlantic*, June 2011, 66.

8. OECD stands for The Organization for Economic Co-operation and Development, the organization that proctors standardized tests for the government.

9. Arne Duncan, *New York Times*, December 7, 2010.

10. Arne Duncan, *Time Magazine*, September 20, 2010, 42.

11. Arne Duncan, remarks at the National Alliance for Public Charter Schools Conference, June 2009.

12. Klein, "Scenes from the Class Struggle," The Atlantic, June 2011, 73.

13. See, for example, Geoffrey Canada, "Bringing Change to Scale: The Next Big Reform Challenge," in *Waiting for Superman*, 190.

14. *Waiting for Superman* is a film by David Guggenheim and Lesley Chilcott, Paramount Vantage and Participant Media, in association with Walden Mediak, 2010.

15. Ann Bastian, et al, *Choosing Equality: The Case for Democratic Schooling* (Philadelphia: Temple University Press, 1986), 24.

16. Ken Goodman, "More Children Left Behind," in *Saving Our Schools: The Case for Public Education Saying No To "No Child Left Behind,"* ed. K. Goodman, P. Shannon, Y. Goodman, and R. Rapoport (Berkeley, CA: RDR Books, 2004), 161.

17. Christopher Robbins, *Expelling Hope: The Assault on Youth and the Militarization of Schooling* (Albany: SUNY Press, 2008), 161.

18. See the work of Lisa Delpit, especially *Other People's Children: Cultural Conflict in the Classroom* (New York: The New Press, 1995).

19. See Patricia Hill Collins, *Another Kind of Public Education: Race, Schools, the Media and Democratic Possibilities* (Boston: Beacon, 2010).

20. Patrick Finn, *Literacy with an Attitude: Educating Working Class Children in Their Own Best Interests* (Albany: SUNY Press, 1999), 185.

21. Original, previously unpublished quote.

22. Jacqueline Ancess, *Beating the Odds: High Schools as Communities of Commitment* (New York: Teachers College Press, 2003), 121.

23. Alfie Kohn, "When '21st-Century Schooling' Just Isn't Good Enough: A Modest Proposal," *Rethinking Schools* 23, no. 3 (Spring 2009).

24. Abigail and Stephan Thernstrom, *No Excuses: Closing the Racial Gap in Learning* (New York: Simon and Schuster, 2003), 75.

25. John Dewey, *Democracy and Education* (New York: Barnes and Noble, 2005), 192.

26. Original quote, previously unpublished.

27. Pedro Noguera, *City Schools and the American Dream: Reclaiming the Promise of American Education* (New York: Teachers College Press, 2003), 23.

Chapter One

The New Three *Rs*: Relay Race Reform

Unpacking the Language of Twenty-first Century School Reform and Policy

The path to success has never been clearer. The educational reform movement is not a table where we all sit around and talk. It's a train that is leaving the station, gaining speed, momentum, and direction. It is time for everyone, everywhere to get on board.
—Arne Duncan, remarks at the National Alliance for Public Charter Schools Conference, June 2009

This chapter summarizes and analyzes of some of the mandates, rhetoric, and ideologies guiding school-reform policy in the twenty-first century, providing context and contrast for the chapters that follow. Before discussing some highly innovative schools that exemplify the concept of *embracing risk*, it is important to understand the broader cultural, political, and economic landscape in which these schools operate. It is easy to see these schools in terms of their successes, and to highlight the ways in which they are creatively resculpting pedagogy and practice. But in many ways these schools are more than simply innovative; they are actively *oppositional*.

These schools are taking enormous risks by going against the grain at a time when public education is increasingly under a microscope, and when the stakes for federal funding and support are increasingly competitive, prescribed, and nonnegotiable. The quote above from Arne Duncan suggests that the fundamentally democratic process of discussion and debate (e.g., having educational stakeholders sit around the table and "talk" to each other) is essentially a waste of time. According to Duncan, school reform is not a communal process; it is a fast-moving train that knows exactly where it's going and has no time to waste getting there. There is but one directive: *get on board.*

The language of No Child Left Behind may be slightly more appealing (at least, more inclusive) than Duncan's speeding train metaphor, but both suggest that education is a kind of race where everybody must run in the same direction, toward the same endpoint. In the term *Race to the Top*, which currently guides American school-funding policy, there isn't even a child at all. States are competing against each other for limited funding (there isn't room at "the top" for everyone), a system that is producing crafty winners and embittered losers. Moreover, the race to the top has become America's race for superiority and superpower status in a world where we are quickly being "out-educated."

This chapter takes a close look at some of the assumptions underpinning the push toward greater standardization and scripting of curricula, high-stakes national testing, value-added measures (VAM) of teacher accountability, and competitive and market models of school funding, leadership, and organization. Looking at the language contemporary educators, educational policy makers, and educational funders commonly use to talk about school reform and public education, it becomes clear that there are significant disagreements surrounding what constitutes a "successful" school, a "good" teacher, a "rigorous" curriculum, and "accurate" assessment of student learning. Though such debates are certainly not new, they have taken on a new sense of urgency, become increasingly polarizing and authoritarian.

Consider, for example, the following excerpt from a speech by Duncan as he considers the fate of chronically underperforming schools [emphasis mine]: "States and districts have a *legal obligation* to *hold administrators and teachers accountable, demand change* and, where necessary, *compel it.* They have a *moral obligation* to do *the right thing* for *those* children—*no matter how painful and unpleasant.*"[1]

In just two sentences, Duncan makes it obvious what schools are up against when they explicitly challenge the definition of "the right thing" for "those children": legal battles, personal embarrassment, demands for change (backed up by threats to compel it), and accusations of moral depravity regarding children in need. Duncan presents the mandate for reform in such a manner as to suggest that educators who disagree with it are somehow acting cowardly, putting the material needs of special interest groups—such as teachers, unions, and administrators—before those of children.

As I suggested in the introduction, the competitive, relay-race model of school reform is especially effective because it capitalizes upon people's genuine fears, concerns, and lived experiences—especially with regard to the national economy, equal opportunity, and social mobility. For example, many of the policies and slogans discussed in this chapter—such as No Child

Left Behind and "No Excuses"—are steeped in ideologies constructed to appeal to a common vision of equality of opportunity, meritocracy, and other cherished democratic principles. They also appeal to the idea that we now live in a "colorblind" society where discrimination and segregation are no longer an issue. "No Excuses" schools explicitly suggest that *anyone* who works hard and plays by the same rules will necessarily have the same opportunities and rewards.

Upon close examination, however, it becomes clear that, behind the rhetoric of social justice, many of the arguments for public-school reform are carefully constructed to promote the interests of specific stakeholder groups over others. What seems like an attempt to shatter the status quo actually serves to reify and strengthen it. And it's not an exaggeration to suggest that many reformers push toward a system of public education that is no longer even *public*. Many of the entities that are given control over "failing schools" are for-profit companies that use advertising and other consumer products in the classroom.

Yet, as Michael Apple reminds us: "The first thing to ask about an ideology is not what is false about it, but what is true. What are its connections to lived experience? Ideologies, properly conceived, do not dupe people. To be effective, they must connect to real problems, real experiences."[2] Thus, *until we seriously attempt to understand how particular ideologies about school reform have been consciously and methodically manipulated to win popular support, we have little leverage to challenge and change them.*

Specifically, this chapter explores popular ideologies around: (1) the purpose and need for public education; (2) the process of school reform; (3) the value and role of teachers and school leaders; (4) student and school-based assessment; (5) how to deal with underperforming schools; and (6) how to close the achievement gap for "at-risk" and underserved children.

BUT FIRST: A SURPRISE QUIZ!

1) Vocabulary and Logic

Compare and contrast the following statements:

> Data gives us the roadmap to reform. It tells us where we are, where we need to go, and who is most at risk. . . . Data may not tell the whole truth, but it certainly doesn't lie.
> —Secretary of Education Arne Duncan[3]

> If the facts don't fit the theory, change the facts.
> —Albert Einstein

In your analysis, consider the following questions: What is the difference, both in theory and in practice, between "lying" and "not telling the whole truth"? How might they become confused? Likewise, when Einstein suggests "changing the facts" to fit the theory, is he, in fact, advocating a kind of cheating or trickery? What else might he be implying by this statement? Finally, regardless of their motivation, can you think of concrete ways that administrators and teachers may succeed in changing the facts (e.g., manipulating the results of high-stakes test scores)?

2) Short Answer

The following remarks were made to students on their first day at North Star Charter School by the school's co-founder James Verrilli: "This school is all about choice. . . . See that back door? See any locks on it? Is this a prison? Am I forcing you to be here? . . . If you cannot live by our rules, if you cannot adapt to this place, I can show you the back door."[4]

Why do you think Verrilli suggests that students who disagree with school rules should have to leave, and especially to leave by "the back door"? Why shouldn't they be able to leave through the front door? What does the back door exit convey to students about their actual freedom of choice?

3) Logic/Statistics/Semantics

According to Eric Hanushek, senior fellow at Stanford University: "Teachers near the top of the quality distribution can get an entire year's worth of additional learning out of their students compared to those near the bottom."[5]

What does Hanushek mean when he talks of "the quality distribution," and what are the implications of referring to teachers—complex human beings—as if they are a manufactured product? Also, how do you think Hanushek determined/measured the statistic that top-quality teachers could get "an entire year's worth" of additional learning out of their students? Finally, what does it say about the process of learning when it is referred to as something teachers "get out of" their students?

4) Vocabulary and Logic

According to an editorial in the *New York Times* regarding a proposed bill that would allow districts to fire teachers based on performance rather than seniority:

> The Legislature must make sure that the scoring system weighs student performance most heavily, so that unfit teachers aren't allowed to remain on the job by performing well in peripheral areas.[6]

How would you define what constitutes "peripheral areas"? Before answering, consider the following: Does peripheral areas include all subjects not currently on the state test (e.g., history, science, art, etc.)? Likewise, does peripheral include everything not strictly related to transmitting content knowledge, for example: (1) building trusting/mentoring relationships with students; (2) helping students and their families find social services that will ultimately improve their performance in school; (3) mediating potentially contentious or violent situations; (4) collaborating with other teachers to enrich and improve practice?

5) Short Answer/Opinion

According to Secretary of Education Duncan, teachers "want to know exactly what they need to do to teach and how to teach. It makes their job easier. . . . They aren't guessing or talking in generalities anymore. They feel as if they're starting to crack the code."[7]

Do you believe that there is a "code" for good teaching? Consider, for example, whether good teaching is the same across all contexts and cultures. Can you think of reasons that some teachers might resent being told "exactly what they need to teach and how to teach" rather than viewing it as something that "makes their job easier"?

6) Short Answer

A *Philadelphia Inquirer* editorial titled "Bias Trumps Choice" profiles the Eversham School District's seven-to-two vote against participating in the state's interdistrict-choice program, which would force it to enroll up to sixty-three students from other (poorer) school districts. The editorial states:

> Residents of Burlington County town said they were worried that their property values would go down if a group of mostly minority, poor kids suddenly started matriculating in Eversham's schools.[8]

• What can you infer from this editorial about the viability of vouchers/ redistricting as a means of providing school choice and closing the achievement gap?
• What are some of the implied consequences of a system that ties school funding to property taxes?

7) Metaphor

> What we need are teachers who don't make excuses. I don't want to hear about bureaucracy. We have always had bureaucracies. We are looking for people who say, "I can teach a rock to read." If it is not the right place for you, then you should find another place to go. —urban school district superintendent[9]

What does this superintendent really mean or imply when she uses the metaphor "teach a rock to read?" In your opinion, is this metaphor meant to be taken positively (all children can succeed), or is it a kind of insult (comparing the intelligence of some children to that of a rock)?

8) Agree/Disagree

According to Gregory Hodge, head of the Frederick Douglas Academy, "responsibility" is "a middle-class value."[10]

Do you agree that responsibility is a "middle-class" value? Explain your reasoning. What does your argument suggest about working-class and poor people in America?

9) Equations/Logic

According to the daily chant used at KIPP charter schools:

> The more you read,
> The more you know.
> Knowledge is power.
> Power is money, and
> I *want* it.[11]

1. How would you note this theory in the form of an equation?
2. How can you prove it to be true? In your analysis, consider all extenuating circumstances such as *reading without understanding, knowledge that is decontextualized and essentially meaningless, knowledge that is purposefully silenced or marginalized,* and *social and legal systems* that prevent people from gaining power and money even when they are knowledgeable.
3. What other purposes might motivate people to become knowledgeable besides wanting power or money?

10) Short Answer/Analysis

According to Secretary of Education Duncan:

> Closing underperforming schools may seem like a surrender, but in some cases it's the only responsible thing to do. It instantly improves the learning conditions for those kids and brings a failing school to a swift and thorough conclusion.[12]

1. List and explain the ways that closing underperforming schools "instantly" improves the learning conditions for "those kids."

2. Can you think of circumstances in which closing a public neighborhood school might be harmful to "those kids" and to their communities? For example, schools might be a source of highly needed public meeting spaces, social services, childcare, safe spaces, or community pride. Explain your answer.
3. When Duncan talks of bringing schools to a "swift and thorough conclusion," what other kinds of objects is Duncan comparing schools to (e.g., a novel, a legal trial), and do these comparisons hold true?

11) Logic Problems

Explain the logic behind the following statements and, if you disagree with either statement, *rewrite it* in a way that makes more sense to you:

> Good schooling must come before parental support, not the other way around.[13]
> —Jay Mathews, author and educational columnist for the *Washington Post*

> Failed schools equal failed communities, and successful schools equal thriving communities.[14] —Bill Strickland, CEO, Manchester Bidwell Corporation

12) True or False

Which of the following statements are absolutely true? How can you prove or disprove them? What variables might cause you to rethink you assumptions?

1. More time in school = more learning = more meaningful learning
2. More time in school = more time "on-task" = better test scores
3. More time in school = harder work = increased personal motivation
4. More time in school = increased personal motivation = increased probability of individual success

13) Short Answer

After reading the following two descriptions of real urban public schools, respond to the supposition by many educational reformers that "money doesn't matter." Can you think of ways in which the environments described below might have a significant impact on students' concentration, motivation, and even test scores?

> The school is so old that rain enters the classrooms through leaky roofs. The paint is peeling off the walls and you could get sick from that because it could be poisonous. The floor makes a weird noise and some of our tables have holes. . . . Sometimes the heater doesn't work and we have to spend at least a

week in a school with no heat. Sometimes the electricity goes out and we have to spend at least two days without school. . . . Also the ceilings have cracks in them and sometimes dust just falls right out from them onto us in class.[15]

Ninety-six percent of our kids are of Mexican descent. . . . The majority are first or second generation immigrants. We're extremely overcrowded. The school was built for 800 students, but we're up to almost 1500 now. . . . We have eight mobile units in the parking lot out back. . . . Due to overcrowding . . . my classroom would be a converted coat closet.[16]

14) Agree/Disagree?

Florida governor Rick Scott is quoted as saying that: "Good teachers know they don't need tenure. There is no reason to have it expect to protect those that don't perform as they should."[17]

As you answer, consider if there are other reasons might teachers want to support tenure (as well as unionization and collective bargaining) besides protecting themselves when they know they are performing poorly?

15) Short Answer

First, read the following commentary by school teacher Christopher Paslay, author of *The Village Proposal*:

Public school officials must make a choice. Do they want schools to be nothing more than shelters for troubled children who have nowhere else to go? Or do they want them to institutions of learning where hardworking children can get an education and become productive members of society?

If they want the former, the district should shift its focus from instruction to social services that address basic needs, such as citizenship and conflict resolution. If they want the latter, then they have to enact discipline policies that expedite the remediation and removal of students who continue to rob others of their right to learn.[18]

Do you think that Paslay is correct in assuming that public officials must "make a choice" between these two options? Are they the only two options? Is there any way to combine them? For example, in what ways do you think educating children to be productive members of society also depends on teaching about and addressing *citizenship* and *conflict resolution*?

16) Agree or Disagree?

The greatest problem facing African Americans is their isolation from the tacit norms of the dominant culture.[19] —sociologist Orlando Patterson

As you explain your reasoning, be sure to identify what you think Patterson means by the terms *isolation, tacit norms*, and *dominant culture*. Additionally, do you think this same statement is equally relevant for other minority or nondominant groups besides African Americans? Why or why not?

17) Logic/Short Answer

According to *New York Times* columnist Bob Herbert:

> Long years of evidence show that poor kids of all ethnic backgrounds do better academically when they go to school with their more affluent—that is, middle-class—peers. . . . If you really want to improve the education of poor children, you have to get them away from learning environments that are smothered by poverty.[20]

In this statement, Herbert seems to be suggesting that integrating poor kids attending poor schools into more affluent schools populated by more affluent families is a good strategy for boosting their academic achievement. Compare this to an alternative theory: helping kids in poverty-stricken schools by improving the schools from within, including greater funding, material resources, community/business partnerships, professional-development opportunities, and other support systems. What are the pros and cons of these very different approaches?

18) Short Answer

Responding to projections that most schools will not reach 100 percent proficiency for all student groups in 2014 (as mandated by No Child Left Behind), former secretary of education Margaret Spellings said:

> These are the achievement targets they promised. It's been stall, stall, stall, and now what, we're going to hit the reset button on the accountability clock?[21]

In your opinion, did schools have a choice when they made this "promise" to reach full proficiency by 2014? What *resources* were they given to help them fulfill this promise? Is *stall* the correct word to describe what schools have been doing and why they have not reached proficiency? Finally, what are the implications of thinking of accountability in terms of an alarm clock (i.e., something that has a set deadline and endpoint rather than an ongoing human process)?

UNPACKING THE ASSUMPTIONS

Rather than the typical multiple-choice format that (supposedly) has one and only one correct answer, these questions require critical analysis, combined with personal opinion, politics, theories of change, and logic. I include them here because I hope you will consider sharing them with your colleagues and, where appropriate, with your students as well. I hope that they guide and provoke significant discussion and debate about issues that are central to our public schools and to the value of education itself, as well as the principles of equity inherent in American democracy.

Instead of providing "answers" then, this chapter concludes with an overview of some of the assumptions that are implicit in the questions above— *assumptions that the schools profiled in chapters 2 through 5 challenge in both theory and action.*

Assumption: It's OK to talk about American public schools—which involve complex social relationships, engaged learning, community and culture building, and creativity and innovation—as static objects that can be scientifically rated, replicated, or condemned. Within this framework, students are likened to products that are judged on one-time "performances" (e.g., high-stakes tests) or as dense but malleable objects, such as rocks (e.g., you can "teach a rock to read"). Likewise teachers are compared to a machine, much like a computer or coffeemaker, that can be scientifically ranked, easily outdated or upgraded, and that performs a relatively singular, isolated function (hold and display data, make coffee, etc.).

Assumption: Schools that do not perform well—as measured almost entirely by adequate yearly progress on state test scores—should be radically restructured in a top-down fashion or converted to charters or privately run institutions. Barring that, they should be completely closed down. This assumption is closely linked to the ideas that: (1) when a failing school is closed that there are always "better" and "available" choices for students and families accessible in the surrounding community; (2) other than testing, schools do not provide social services that communities depend on; and (3) closing schools "swiftly" (i.e., without a lot of thought, community input, or planning) is the best course of action even if it leaves a lot of families puzzled, frightened, and feeling ashamed.

Assumption: Data collected from standardized and state test scores should drive major funding and policy decisions about public education, even though it has been proved repeatedly how misleading and easily manipulated this data can be. For example: teachers may teach directly to the test and marginalize all other subjects; states may change the tests to make them easier to pass; teachers may focus all their attention on students *just below* proficiency; teachers might reward "good" students with material prizes for studying and attending school the day of the test; teachers may suspend or push out "poor" students who will bring down the median scores.

Assumption: Teachers are either "good" or "bad" at their jobs, and this is something that we can objectively measure by students' yearly test scores in narrowly selected subject areas. Many people believe that teachers can and should be judged independently of the vastly different contexts in which they work (e.g., class size) and resources available to them (texts, computers, assistant teachers, libraries, planning time, professional development opportunities, etc.). Moreover, it is argued that measurement of teachers should not take into consideration their so-called "peripheral" skills, which are commonly defined as anything that is not "teaching to the test." It should also be noted that, in many cases, teachers have radically different groups of students from year to year (due to high dropout rates, increased public options, and family mobility). Such factors might make it difficult to clearly measure progress within a teacher's classroom from one year to the next.

Assumption: *What students learn and how they perform on tests can be traced directly back to their relationship with a single teacher*, even though students often learn literacy skills in science classes, or math skills in social studies classes. Moreover, in many urban public schools, teacher turnover within the course of the school year is extremely high, making it less likely that students will have a consistent relationship with one teacher.

Assumption: Creating competition among teachers rather than promoting collaboration will benefit schools and students. This is related to the assumption that a sizable number of teachers in failing schools don't really want to improve, that they are lazy and/or are complacent in taking advantage of the system. Thus what is needed to increase their motivation is competition in the form of narrow accountability, decreased job security, and publication of their students' test scores without additional context. This assumption must be considered against significant research that that most people who become teachers do not do so for the prestige or money involved, but rather for a genuine love of children and learning, and a desire to create a better future.

Assumption: It's OK for "good" teachers to resort to increasing student achievement by threats or bribes. It is assumed that there is no difference between student motivation under these circumstances and *genuine* motivation that comes from innate curiosity and desire to know more, as well as the understanding that what they are doing in school is useful and relevant to their lives, values, cultures, communities, and futures.

Assumption: The more time students spend physically confined in the school building, the more time students spend "on-task," and the greater the quantity of knowledge (facts) they amass. The biggest problem with this assumption is that being in school does not necessarily mean that students are

doing something productive. Just because students can be found sitting quietly at desks for long periods of time does not necessarily mean they are
carefully listening, interested, understanding, or otherwise engaged.

*Assumption: The United States is a true meritocracy where individual
hard work and willpower is all that is needed to overcome legal and structu-
ral inequalities, and where success and social mobility is predicated primarily on individual effort and talent. This assumption is made popular in the
phrase "there are no shortcuts" to success.* Most disadvantaged children,
however, know, from years of experience and from members of their family,
that this is at best an oversimplification and often a downright lie. The rich
and powerful have always had "shortcuts," either in the form of open and
legally sanctioned inequities, or in the form of back-room handshakes,
bribes, favoring children of alumni, and so on. As Pedro Noguera says:
"While effort is a key ingredient in individual success, for those who are born
poor it is not a guarantee."[22]

*Assumption: "Good schooling must come before parental support, not the
other way around" and "Failed schools equal failed communities and successful schools equal thriving communities."* The idea here is that parents
need not be genuinely involved in imagining, creating, fighting for, and
sustaining good schools in their communities, but rather that they constitute
the "clientele" that schools are created to serve. Likewise, if schools fail to
adequately serve this clientele, communities are essentially helpless to step in
and intervene. In this dynamic, not only do community leaders and advocates
have nothing to bring to the process of school reform, but the schools (one
institution) ultimately become a reflection on and prediction of the community's entire worth and future.

Assumption: Money is not a key ingredient in successful school reform.
Here, the material condition of schools and working conditions of teachers
and students are essentially irrelevant. If schools are severely overcrowded,
do not have accessible bathrooms or heat in the winter, if the air itself is toxic
to students, or the building's infrastructure is unsafe, this is considered a
shame but not a deal-breaker. It should not, in other words, have a profound
impact on students' ability to learn and to compete. This also means that the
system of funding public schools based on property taxes (where schools
receive differentials as vast as $3,000 and $20,000 per student) may be
problematic, but it does not need to be an integral part of the solution.

*Assumption: "Disadvantaged" kids do best when they leave their home
cultures at home, make them invisible, and/or get rid of them altogether.*
While rarely stated this bluntly, much school-reform rhetoric suggests that
schooling should be about a process of assimilation to what are perceived as
white, middle-class values (e.g., responsibility, speech and dress codes, etc.).
While there is substance to the argument that when students leave schools

these "values" will have an impact on future opportunities, the goal of schools is that of blind acculturation, rather than teaching students to become literate in and/or critically assess and challenge these values.

Assumption: Schools that focus on issues of citizenship, conflict mediation, problem-solving, and social justice, and so on are necessarily weak in academic content and vigor. The assumption here is that schools cannot accomplish *both* civic and academic goals, and that, furthermore, they are not even related. This ignores the many innovative and successful ways that teachers have sought to connect teaching about specific content knowledge with open discussion and debate; hands-on experimental, inquiry-based learning; collaborative learning; and real-world problem-solving.

Assumption: School reform is a sequential event with a single goal and clear endpoint or summit (e.g., in No Child Left Behind, *all students are to be proficient in math and reading by the year 2014).* This stands in stark contrast to the idea that schools are a constantly changing, living community made up of unique individuals, opportunities, and conflicting ideas and ideals. And one must ask the question: even if all students were deemed proficient in math and reading by the year 2014, what does this guarantee about the years 2015 and beyond? *In other words, is proficiency a one-time, nonrenewable event?*

Assumption: Teachers actually prefer heavily mandated and scripted curricula that takes the "guesswork" out of their jobs. This assumption is very dominant, despite the fact that many teachers continually argue the opposite—that part of what attracts teachers to the profession is the ability to use their creativity, curiosity, and performance skills to demonstrate empathy, care and compassion for individual children, and to rise to unplanned "teachable moments" generated by current events or children themselves. Indeed, many teachers are leaving the profession precisely because they feel they have no autonomy, are treated like robots, and are being held accountable for factors that they do not buy into or can't control.

Assumption: Students who disagree with school rules or question established school practices need to learn to "hold their tongue" or be asked to leave in disgrace (e.g., through the back door). Such a practice defies the democratic principles of free speech, shared leadership, and individualism that schools need to model for students. Moreover, it is rarely suggested that students should have a genuine stake in developing such rules and being active members of the school's governing and decision-making bodies. In many cases, school leaders believe the best way to deal with so-called "miscreant" students is to overpower and humiliate them. Some "No Excuses" schools say that "you can't argue your way to privilege," suggesting that you are either worthy of privilege or not, but speaking up for your rights is certainly not the best course of action.

Assumption: Getting students out of poverty (one by one) is a more important goal, and must precede, any attempts to dismantle systems of poverty, discrimination, and inequity. Teachers are encouraged to "get students out of the ghetto," rather than work collectively to help find the resources needed to enrich the "ghetto" or to challenge the assumptions behind the label "ghetto." In other words, encouraging students to challenge and work toward changing the *status quo* turns public schools into ideological and political institutions. The belief that public schools are already political institutions is generally ignored.

Assumption: Because school choice is appealing in theory, we can have confidence that it will actually work in practice. The fact that many good schools do not have room for, or are unwilling to accept, children from failing schools (because, for example, they will bring down the schools' test scores and by association property taxes) is basically considered irrelevant here. Also, it should be noted that "wealthy" and/or "successful" schools that do accept students from other districts often track them in lower-level courses, and/or label them "special education students".

Write any additional assumptions you've uncovered here:

In the following four chapters, I now turn my attention to schools that actively challenge these assumptions on a daily basis. I began this chapter by saying that these schools are, in many ways, oppositional. But it is important to remember that opposition is not limited to rejecting bad ideas and proven misconceptions about education. These are also schools that are constructing *positive alternatives*, proving that there *are* positive alternatives to be discovered. While not every new idea is perfect, the courage to explore radically different approaches to education is the first step toward reform that is not reactionary but visionary. The difference is vital; as Dewey says:

> There is always the danger in a new movement that in rejecting the aims and methods of that which it would supplant, it may develop its principles negatively rather than positively or constructively. Then it takes its clue in practice from that which is rejected instead of from the constructive development of its own philosophy.[23]

NOTES

1. Arne Duncan, remarks at the National Alliance for Public Charter Schools Conference, June 2009.
2. Michael Apple, *Official Knowledge: Democratic Education in a Conservative Age* (New York: Routledge, 1993), 20.

3. Arne Duncan, "Robust Data Gives Us the Roadmap to Reform," addresses the Fourth Annual IES Research Conference, 2009.

4. James Verrilli, in *No Excuses: Closing the Racial Gap in Learning*, ed. Abigail Thernstrom, and Stephen Thernstrom (New York: Simon and Schuster, 2003), 49.

5. Eric Hanushek, "The Difference Is Great Teachers," in *Waiting for Superman: How We Can Save America's Schools* (New York: Public Affairs, 2010), 85.

6. *New York Times*, March 7, 2011.

7. Arne Duncan, "Robust Data Gives Us The Roadmap to Reform."

8. "Bias Trumps Choice," *Philadelphia Inquirer*, October 29, 2010, A18.

9. *The Philadelphia Schools Notebook*, January 26, 2011.

10. Gregory Hodge, in *No Excuses, Closing the Racial Gap in Learning*, 65.

11. KIPP Charter School chant, written by Harriet Ball.

12. Arne Duncan, "Turning Around the Bottom Five Percent," remarks at the National Alliance for Public Charter Schools Conference.

13. Jay Matthews, "What Really Makes a Super School," in *Waiting for Superman*, 173.

14. Bill Strickland, "How Schools Kill Neighborhoods—And Can Help Save Them," in *Waiting for Superman*, 74.

15. Jeff Shultz and Alison Cook-Sather, *In Our Own Words: Students' Perspectives on School* (Lanham, MD: Rowman & Littlefield, 2011), 31.

16. G. Michie, *Holler If You Hear Me: The Education of a Teacher and His Students* (New York: Teachers College Press, 1999), 21.

17. *New York Times*, February 1, 2011.

18. Christopher Paslay, "Less Than 'Zero Tolerance,'" *Philadelphia Inquirer*, January 23, 2011, A19.

19. Orlando Patterson, in *No Excuses, Closing the Racial Gap in Learning*, 79.

20. Bob Herbert "Separate and Unequal," *New York Times*, March 22, 2011.

21. Margaret Spellings, *New York Times*, March 10, 2011.

22. Pedro Noguera, *City Schools and the American Dream: Reclaiming the Promise of American Education* (New York: Teachers College Press, 2003), 13.

23. John Dewey, *Experience and Education* (New York: Free Press, 1997), 20.

Chapter Two

A Mission to Question: Inquiry, Creativity, and Risk

The Science Leadership Academy (SLA)

Acquiring is always secondary, and instrumental to the act of inquiring.
—John Dewey[1]

When I hear people say it's our job to create the twenty-first century work-force, it scares the hell of me. . . . Our job is to create twenty-first century citizens. We need workers, yes, but we also need scholars, activists, parents—compassionate, engaged people. We're not reinventing schools to create a new version of a trade school. We're reinventing schools to help kids be adaptable in a world that is changing at a blinding rate.
—Science Leadership Academy founding principal Christopher Lehmann

When Christopher Lehmann came up with the idea of asking the Philadel-phia School District to let him develop and start a new public high school, which would eventually become the Science Leadership Academy (SLA), he turned the idea of inquiry-based education on its head. Working in close partnership with the city's renowned science museum, The Franklin Institute, Lehmann envisioned a high school that would use the methodologies primar-ily associated with progressive science education across the entire curricu-lum. The spirit of curiosity, creating one's own hypotheses and questions, and active experimentation would become part of the five core values that guide every *learning experience at the SLA: inquiry, collaboration, research, presentation, and reflection.*

Inquiry and project-based learning, a process which typically incorporates all five of these values, would become the school's primary pedagogy. Moreover, the projects that students would engage in would be rooted in real-world issues, cross disciplinary boundaries, and involve multiple cycles of the five core values—always returning to the first value: student inquiry.

The SLA embraces risk by requiring its students to ask challenging, provocative, and sometimes uncomfortable or game-changing questions as part of the very process of learning. Rather than measuring student achievement and success in terms of students' ability to memorize and retain facts and information, the SLA has created a curriculum and school culture in which students must put knowledge into action.

This means that most assignments end with students creating something new or testing an experimental hypothesis, followed by critical reflection on the impact of their actions. The school's main ideology is best expressed by Freire: "To teach is not to transfer knowledge but create the possibilities for the production or construction of knowledge."

THE SLA AT A GLANCE

- Entire school, including mission statement, built on value of sustained inquiry.
- Focus on project-based, problem-solving learning, often resulting in student creations or recommendations that can be shared, used, or replicated in real life.
- Agreed-upon "core values" sequentially integrated into all curricula: inquiry, collaboration, research, presentation, and reflection.
- Community partnership with local science museum, serving as extension of school/classroom space and opportunity for students to go "backstage," help create exhibits, and guide visitors.
- Emphasis on student leadership, including opportunities for students to participate in building the school community itself (such as interviewing prospective teachers and students, and serving as assistant teachers).
- In-service and Independent Learning Projects (ILPs) as part of the curriculum, letting students integrate school-based learning with work in the community, and explore individual interests.
- Using new technologies in innovative ways to promote student learning, as well as to enable collaboration, social networking, and expanded opportunities for creativity and self-expression.

- Demographics: 48 percent African American, 38 percent Caucasian, 7 percent Latina, 7 percent Asian, 1 percent other; 50 percent economically disadvantaged; students come from over eighty different feeder schools from every zip code in the city.

A Mission to Question

- How do we learn?
- What can we create?
- What does it mean to lead?

When you go to the website of Philadelphia's Science Leadership Academy and click on "mission," you are faced with these three questions. The expectation, given that this is a supposed to be a mission *statement*, is that the website will answer these questions for you. It doesn't. They hang there, challenging, provocative, open-ended.

Why create a mission statement composed of questions?

A school mission that begins with questions invites dialogue and debate, imagination and innovation. A mission statement that begins with questions suggests that the process of education in this school is not a static one, nor is it decided by the vision and leadership of one person, stakeholder group, or organization. The SLA invites students, teachers, administrators, parents, and community members to contribute to and actively engage in the school's mission every time they encounter and consider these three questions.

What of the questions themselves?

On the surface these seem like reasonable questions for an educational institution to ask. And yet, as I have noted before,[2] they rarely are posed in this format because, in contrast to the ideology of "No Excuses," such questions carry significant risks. Asking "How do we learn?" for example, suggests that learning is more complicated than the traditional method of lecture, memorization, and testing. It leaves open the possibility that different people learn in different ways, and suggests that there are numerous sources of knowledge beyond those found in traditional classrooms and textbooks.

This question also suggests that the *process* of learning, rather than simply the *product* of learning, is important. It raises questions about the assumption that learning is a one-directional process (flowing from teacher to student) and that knowledge is something that teachers either "put into" or "get out of" students. It also suggests that there may be more than one right answer, perspective or approach to solving problems, and that our answers to any questions may change according to the frameworks and contexts in which they are asked.

Asking "What can we create?" is also a provocative question in the current educational climate, which highly privileges student knowledge as measured by standardized testing. The traditional understanding of learning is that of internalizing a fixed list of data,[3] and demonstrating decontextualized recall of this data in a timed, competitive, and standardized format. To emphasize and value the process of "creation" in school implies that knowledge must be *put to use* to become meaningful.

It further suggests that there are many different ways of "demonstrating" learning and that sometimes the end result of education is not so much grasping a "concept" as initiating a transformation or expanding one's perspective. For example, students are also demonstrating the critical link between learning and creating when they mediate a conflict in their community, organize a fundraiser for a cause they feel passionately about, travel to another country to share resources with and learn more about another culture, or delve more deeply into understanding their own family history and values.

Finally, asking "What does it mean to lead?" suggests that the purpose of school is more than just theoretical or academic (transmitting skills and data in discrete subject areas). The idea that leadership is a quality worth investigating suggests that schools are also social and political sites where students need to practice the decision-making and leadership skills that will sustain and strengthen American democratic ideals as their generation comes of age.

These leadership skills are not limited to the skill of being able to "take charge" and "make a decision"—skills often associated with CEOs of large corporations. Nor is leadership solely about the acquisition of power, winning competitions, or being rewarded or given awards. Effective leaders also need to practice the skills of active listening, shared ownership, empathy, respectful discussion and debate, adaptability, commitment, humility, and courage. SLA nurtures all of these qualities.

The SLA's mission statement uses critical questions about the construction and purpose of learning to suggest that education is an ongoing and sometimes very subjective process. By asking how we create and what it means to lead, the SLA requires its students to think about the *relevance* and *significance* of what they are learning, and what happens when abstract ideas and knowledge need to be applied to real-life problems and opportunities.

INQUIRY-BASED EDUCATION

The SLA's explicit commitment to inquiry-based learning does not mean that *anything goes*. It does not mean that the school has no structure or measurable goals and standards, that students are not regularly assessed and graded, or that teachers do not care about teaching content. Just the opposite is true. By committing to using the SLA core values in each of their lesson plans, teachers have the opportunity to be creative about what and how they teach, while sharing a common vision. At the center of this vision is the idea that students need opportunities to ask critical questions and consider alternatives. While these values, which stress the processes of discovery and exploration, are often identified with the sciences, the SLA presumes that such pedagogy can be used across the disciplines.

At the SLA, student learning and inquiry begins even before students are admitted to the school. When prospective students come to be interviewed, one of the first questions they are asked is: "What will you bring to the SLA community?" And this question is not posed solely by an SLA teacher, but also by the SLA students who volunteer to be part of the admissions process. The idea is that students are among the key stakeholders in the SLA, and as such, they are dedicated to bringing in new students who will continue to support and enrich the school as it grows.

Prospective students are then asked to share a project they did in middle school, exploring both the process and conclusions drawn, but also the ways in which their participation in this project may have changed their initial assumptions, complicated stereotypes, challenged "truths," or raised new questions that need to be investigated further. Students are asked, in other words, to demonstrate their love of learning, a very different process from simply proving their superior intelligence, skills, or competence.

Indeed, students are active in all parts of the schools' organization and leadership structure. They even participate in interviewing and hiring decisions about new teachers. On a practical level, this experience helps students become more invested in the school and in their own educations. But it also lets them think critically about the value and purpose of going to school, and recognize that school is not something being *done to them* so much as *created by them*. Another important part of the SLA's vision is to help students make connections between seemingly unrelated ideas and data sets, and to help students see the purpose and relevance of what they are learning to the kinds of decisions and judgments they must navigate daily.

A Spanish teacher, for example, overheard students in the hallway talking about the latest fad diet. While on the surface the conversation had nothing to do with learning Spanish, she found a teachable moment. She asked to students to blog (in Spanish, of course!) for five days about everything they ate and how much exercise they got. Students were then asked to read each other's blogs and serve as a personal trainer for another student. Even when learning a foreign language, content can be greatly enriched by process and context. Moreover, the concept of "literacy" must include more than simple acts of translation or recall.

In a science class, students were asked to break up into teams, and each team was asked to create and manage its own cell-phone company—cell-phones being a product that teenagers typically use daily. Assignments required students to think about issues across the curriculum, such as the science of building a better phone and upgrading it in response to competitive products, how to price a product for maximum profit and sustainability, and advertising to appeal to different demographics. The goal was not just to engage students in the process of building a business, but to practice working collaboratively, and to pay attention to how one decision inevitably will impact another.

A third example comes from an African American history course (a requirement for all ninth graders in the school district of Philadelphia). Nationally recognized SLA history teacher Gamal Sheriff had his students brainstorm topics from African American history and generate twenty questions they wished to learn more about. Afterward, students reviewed their questions and assigned them to at least one of six possible social institutions: *domestic, economic, education, governmental, judicial,* and *religious.*

They then identified their most pressing questions, and used them to research a topic of their choosing to make a thirty-second "commercial" about a person or event in African American history. Students learned, through firsthand experience, about historical accuracy, point of view, holistic summaries of events, drawing conclusions, citations, and critically analyzing historical documents, including the U.S. Census, the Constitution, and the Bill of Rights.

Sheriff designed this lesson so that students would learn facts and dates important to African American history, while also thinking critically about broader ideas and assumptions connected to civil rights, justice, and historical discourse, such as:

- Civic engagement manifests itself in social institutions;
- Historical artifacts can help people understand and interpret the past, but must themselves be subject to interpretation;
- Evolving laws and culture have changed historical discourse;
- Formal and informal racism are distinct experiences; and
- How present day racial relations are influenced by African American history.

Finally, what could be more relevant to students than studying *their own experiences going to school*? In a senior course titled "Modern Educational Theory," created and taught by the school's principal, Chris Lehmann, students were asked to reflect critically on their own educations and to imagine their "ideal" schools. This meant discussing and debating what qualities and values associated with learning they found most purposeful, useful, and meaningful.

Class readings reflected educational theories across the political spectrum, from E. D. Hirsch to Deborah Meier. After extensive class discussions, Principal Lehmann issued his students the following challenge:

> Now, it is your time to take your stand. You are to write a two-page position paper creating your vision of what school should be. Your paper should consider the following points: Clearly define your vision of school: What is the purpose? Why is it good for the individual? Why is it good for society? What does your vision of school value? Prioritize? Given this vision of school, what differences would you see in the structure of school when compared to a "traditional" school?

The assignment could have stopped here, but Lehmann was sure to include the SLA's core value of *reflection*. Students were asked to share and discuss their school visions, identifying what they believed to be the best part of the vision, and then answering the question: "What is the worst consequence of your best idea?" According to Lehmann, this last question helps students understand that there are no "perfect" ideas when it comes to education. Schools need a strong vision, but this vision cannot be stagnant.

The Museum Experience

SLA students find opportunities to "learn" in many places: the classroom, of course, but also in the community and virtual spaces. For example, SLA was designed in close partnership with The Franklin Institute Science Museum, which serves as a genuine extension of the school building. In ninth grade, all students spend at least one afternoon a week at the museum (as part of a graded course called "The Museum Experience"), where they are able to explore a changing roster of exhibits and museum themes ranging from Galileo to global warming to the science of the brain to computer game design to Cleopatra.

SLA students also have opportunities to learn about the many aspects of working in a museum, including exhibit design, organizing public programs, and educational technology. While they begin with a four-week mini-course in an area of interest, students can eventually commit to year-long internships. Perhaps most significantly, SLA students from all grades can help design and build new exhibits, produce accompanying podcasts, or give tours to other school groups.

While many schools offer occasional class trips to museums, students are not usually privy to what goes on *behind the scenes*. Part of the value (and potential "risk") of this opportunity is that students learn to think critically about how information and sources are chosen, eliminated, or joined together in the curatorial process, and critically deconstruct the process of "framing" and "presenting" historical, scientific, and cultural knowledge. Even when students are not working directly with the Franklin Institute Museum, the school curriculum tries to build on these skills.

One particularly noteworthy assignment comes from SLA history teacher Joshua Block.

As part of a tenth-grade thematic unit on the politics of colonialism, Block assigned each student the task of designing a proposal for a museum exhibit on the impact of colonialism; students were free to choose the country they wanted to research. The proposals would eventually be presented to the board of the (fictional) Museum of Global History (represented by their own classmates), who would decide which exhibits were most deserving of funding and space.

In the process of putting together a formal introduction to the exhibit, choosing their artifacts and writing accompanying text, students were asked to demonstrate an understanding of various aspects of colonialism, such as the rationales behind it, the ways colonialism affected both colonized and colonizer, and the impact of colonialism on the modern world. Students were thus to consider both the *positive* and *negative* impacts of colonialism in the context of the country they had chosen. At the end of their proposals, students were asked to write a "final thoughts" section in which they reflected on what they hoped visitors would see and get out of attending their exhibit as opposed to just reading a history book. Following are two examples of what students came up with:

Example 1:

SLA tenth-grader Catherine focused her exhibit on the colonization of Indonesia by the Dutch. Upon entering the exhibit, visitors will board boats where museum actors, playing the role of Dutch colonizers, take them on a virtual journey to Indonesia. Over the course of the journey, they explain all that the country has to offer and its potential for making other countries rich.

After stepping off the boats, visitors must interact with every "artifact" in the exhibit. In one room, for example, visitors are asked to identify different barrels of spices (a rich resource of Indonesia used not only for cooking but also for medicine and magic potions). This experience is followed by entering a "trading post," a room where visitors sit at tables and negotiate their price.

In the final stages of the exhibit, visitors are forced to choose whether the Dutch were justified in their actions, and to "sit on the side you wish to fight on." Before leaving the exhibit, visitors must navigate through a room full of soldiers fighting the Battle of Java Sea.

Example 2:

SLA tenth-grader Daniel designed a similarly interactive exhibit to demonstrate the impact of colonialism on Niger. The first artifact that visitors are confronted with is a working "treadmill" where they can walk a quarter of a mile. It is then explained that this is a fraction of the distance that some of the country's children now have to go just to get water, as colonialism greatly increased the population and need for resources.

In the next room, visitors are able to walk through two houses, demonstrating the vast differences in lifestyle between the native people (most of whom live in houses made of plastic, trash, and sheets of metal) and wealthier colonizers (who live in cement houses).

Differences in power and money are made visible throughout the experience. At a later stage in the exhibit, for example, Daniel suggests that he will personally "take 61 percent of the people aside and given them each a dollar." He will explain to them that "this represents the 61 percent of the country that lives in poverty with only 1 dollar a day."

EMBRACING NEW TECHNOLOGIES

Since opening five years ago, the SLA has become nationally recognized as a school on the cutting edge of using technology in the classroom. On entering the SLA in ninth grade, each student is issued a Mac computer (theirs for the entire four years), which enables them to use features such as Keynote and iWeb to integrate text, video, and sound into their assignments. Applications like Moodle allow teachers, parents, and students to share homework and benchmark assignments, while technology also facilitates many different forms of collaborative learning and student critique. For example, students can discuss their projects using iChat and communicate on SLA Talk, the school's online bulletin board.

Students can also share their writing and thoughts about what they are learning in school in "real time" with their peers and the general public using the school's blog. A review of recent blog topics underscores the fact that SLA students do not shy away from controversial topics. Recent blog topics include: human trafficking in China; the relationship between joblessness and the homeless; facts and myths about AIDS; the psychological impact of gangs; homosexuality, bullying, and same-sex marriage laws; childhood obesity; child labor, childhood sexual abuse; teen depression and suicide; resisting materialism; the life of a pregnant teen; the impact of school district budget cuts; the relationship among family income, race, and college acceptance; different definitions of democracy; the aftermath of the earthquake in Haiti; the civil war in Libya; wildlife conservation; and domestic violence.

Some blogs are purely about stating the student's opinion on a topic. Others are meant to be informative (e.g., recognizing the signs of teen depression, ways to resist materialism), and others are chronicles meant to help students think about issues in new ways (e.g., the life of a pregnant teen). Many blogs contain concrete suggestions for students who want to make a difference—such as encouraging students to attend rallies on school budget cuts and ways to save animals that are being mistreated.

Lehmann is the creator of an annual conference called EduCon, which is cohosted by the SLA and the Franklin Institute and which draws educators from across the country both in person and virtually. While the three-day event focuses on how to use new technologies in innovative ways across the curricula, it does not bill itself as a "technology conference." It is clearly defined as an *educational* conference. Its guiding principles include:

- Technology must serve pedagogy, not the other way around.
- Technology must enable students to research, create, communicate, and collaborate.
- Learning can—and must—be networked.

Technology at the SLA thus serves not only to make learning more interesting and relevant, but more interactive and more reflective. Perhaps most importantly, the lasting and publicly accessible record created by the online archives of student work, ideas, and innovation means that no project is ever truly "finished." There is always opportunity to insert comments, questions, and new ideas.

THE HEART OF THE SLA: PROJECT-BASED LEARNING

Let's explore two detailed examples of SLA lesson plans that demonstrate how the school has embraced project-based learning—a pedagogy that includes creatively integrated interdisciplinary, intersectional, experiential, multimedia, collaborative, student-centered, and action-based activities. As these examples demonstrate, the result of such a pedagogical approach is learning that ends with new questions, rather than flat answers.

Example 1: Not Just Homework, *Night*work: From Elie Wiesel to "Books Behind Bars" to Improvisational Dance

The Holocaust is an important unit of study in most high-school history classes. Sometimes it is presented to students as part of a historical timeline framed by important wars (e.g., what happened between World War I and the Cold War/Korean War/Vietnam War); at other times, it is presented to students as part of a larger unit on racism, persecution of minorities, uses of power, and the ways in which social movements for justice have had a profound effect on world history.

The Holocaust can be a theme in English/Language Arts classrooms as well, because there are many memoirs, speeches, fictional accounts, and popular films about the Holocaust, written by survivors, perpetrators, witnesses, ancestors of survivors, and more. Perhaps one of the best known such documents is Holocaust survivor Elie Wiesel's book *Night*, along with his Nobel Prize lecture "Hope, Despair and Memory."

At the SLA, tenth-grade English teacher Joshua Block uses Wiesel's *Night* as part of an interdisciplinary approach to studying the Holocaust that combines history and literature, as it raises key questions associated with philosophy, ethics, media studies, legal studies, and public policy analysis. As they learn about the Holocaust, students read a range of *critical essays* and creative writing about the larger themes of imprisonment, society, hope, despair, punishment, and memory.

Eventually, students will be asked to think of and create ways to explore these themes in nonlinguistic forms, such as art or music, and participate in class reenactments and movement studies related to space and freedom. Students also investigate the modern industrial prison complex: they take a class trip to a nearby historical site, the Eastern State Penitentiary, and they get involved in an organization for prisoners called Books Behind Bars.

According to Block, certain essential questions run through all of the components and assignments in this unit of study. For example:

- What does *freedom* mean?
- Does faith help or hurt people facing challenging life situations?
- What is the relationship between our stories, history, and identity?
- To what extent are we all witnesses of history and messengers to humanity?

Likewise, Block created this lesson plan with the hope of furthering student understandings, such as:

- People can use many different strategies to survive difficult situations;
- Imprisonment has profound effects on people;
- Prisons can serve different goals (ranging from punishment to rehabilitation).

Students explore similarities and connections between the events Wiesel writes about and significant issues in their own lives, communities, and across the globe. They select and chart selected quotes from the novel regarding larger themes of *faith*, *relationships*, and *hope* (as well as a theme of their own choosing); when they do this, they must go beyond the literal meaning of the quote to construct a "deep question" that it raises.

Moreover, as students read *Night*, they keep regular journals and respond to a range of writing prompts pertaining to the book generally or to specific passages. The prompts require students to do much more than demonstrate *understanding* and recall of what they read; they must creatively connect ideas and issues raised in the book to other contexts and historical controversies. Prompts included "What is the book bringing up for you?" and "Never shall I forget."

Students are also asked to comment on specific passages in unusual ways, such as "Write down sensory images in this passage," "Consider what things that are changing and things that are staying the same in this passage," and "What kind of connections can you make between this passage and the experience of school?" Students thus must show that they've read the text closely, but also that they can think critically about history and its contemporary relevance. Questions were designed to help students think about how they might have responded in a similar situation, as well as how different ideologies become more or less compelling. For example, students responded to the following questions:

- Consider the larger themes of *Indoctrination/Literacies of Power*: How can you explain that adults weren't willing to listen to what the twelve-year-old was saying? In your opinion, what different things prevent people from seeing or believing the truth?
- Overall what can you say about Nazi indoctrination? What made it so powerful? Would it have been possible to resist it?

In addition to reading the texts and sharing their journals, students took part in various reenactments and other activities about space and expression, with the goal of helping them not only to understand what Wiesel is writing about *intellectually*, but to think about what it would *feel like* to experience similar conditions themselves. For example, in response to Wiesel's description of a crowded prison, Block appointed two students to be the "security guards," and, as he read aloud from the book, commanded the students to move closer and closer together, eventually giving up their "rights" to personal space and freedom of movement.

Another time, Block asked students to work in groups to pick a quote from the book and then portray the quote in *physical movements* rather than *words*. As the quotes were read aloud, students arranged and rearranged themselves into bodily positions, interactions, and expressions to describe the emotions that characters—ranging from prisoners to spectators—were feeling.

One day, Block highlighted a section in the book where a character played Beethoven's violin concerto as his dying act. Block then played a recording of the concerto for the students. He discussed the *literal* format of a "concerto" (one instrument playing to an orchestra and the orchestra's response) and asked them to consider what this might have meant for the prisoner *metaphorically*. Then he asked them: "What would *your* song of freedom or individuality be?" The students brought in, played, and discussed the pieces of music they chose.

For their final projects in the unit on *Night*, students created an art project "that could accompany a future edition of the book." Suggested projects included original drawings, poems, and photographs; they could also create a short graphic novel or design a CD and song list. When students brought in their final projects, they arranged them through the classroom as a kind of "museum exhibit." Thus they had to think not only about the themes and content of the projects, but also about "curating" or framing an exhibit and being *reflective spectators* of each other's work.

To contrast memoir with other kinds of narrative writing, students also read Wiesel's Nobel Prize lecture, "Hope, Despair and Memory." Like *Night*, this speech raises critical issues about the relationship among hope, memory, and active resistance to injustice. Students were asked to carefully read, explain, and respond to complex statements by Wiesel, such as:

- "The opposite of the past is not the future but the absence of future; the opposite of the future is not the past but the absence of the past. The loss of one is equivalent to the sacrifice of the other."
- "And yet it is surely human to forget, even to want to forget. . . . Indeed if memory helps us to survive, forgetting allows us to go on living. How could we go on with our daily lives, if we remained constantly aware of the dangers and ghosts surrounding us? . . . How are we to reconcile our supreme duty towards memory with the need to forget that is essential to life?"

- "We thought it would be enough to tell the tidal wave of hatred which broke over the Jewish people for men everywhere to decide once and for all to put an end to hatred of anyone that was "different." . . . We tried. It was not easy. At first because of the language; language failed us. We would have to invent a new vocabulary, for our words were inadequate, anemic. And then too, the people around us refused to listen, and even those who listened refused to believe, and even those who believed could not comprehend."

Finally, students responded to Wiesel's concluding comments: "There may be times when we are powerless to prevent injustice, but there must never be a time when we fail to protest."

At the same time, students read a variety of contemporary texts, such as a *New York Times* article by Daniel Goleman titled, "The Torturer's Mind: Complex View Emerges."[4] Goleman prompts students to think about how people end up participating in regimes of cruelty and torture, which, he emphasizes, have been common throughout world history. He raises questions such as: "What circumstances can lead someone who may well consider himself a decent person to commit inhumane acts?"

Analyzing torture as part of an ideology of obedience and approval, Goleman suggests, for example, that many torturers see themselves as "guardian[s] of the social good" who believe in "unquestioning obedience to authority" and think they have "the open or tacit support" of their peers. Block uses this as an opportunity to open discussion about the creation and manipulation of an "us vs. them" mentality, along with scapegoating of other humans, as a justification for seemingly indefensible acts.

As students were reading these texts, Block took advantage of a community resource, the Eastern State Penitentiary (a former prison that is now a historic site and museum used to teach the public about the historic conditions of incarceration). Students visited the prison, which is within walking distance of the school, bringing guided research questions about its history and significance. On returning to the classroom, they viewed letters and artwork about men in prison (collected in an anthology by the nonprofit group Books through Bars). As one student reflected on this assignment:

> I never knew the crazy statistics that they had for prisons. I also never knew they had a book program for them. Because the media never showed the fact they wanted to read they would only show the fights, or the way the guards would beat on the prisoners. Never how they wanted to read or how they would make this beautiful art work! I was amazed to find out all this and now my views on prisons have changed so very much.

Students also went to a website, www.360degrees.org, where they read stories of famous and ordinary prisoners; they were asked to "record three things you learned about prisons, prisoners, crime and the criminal justice system in America." This website also let students take online quizzes designed to make them think about how we define a *criminal* and to consider where they stand on a range of contested ethical issues, like stealing when you are needy or taking revenge. Students were then asked to write down their theories of what defines different types of crimes and why people do them, as well as to refute contrasting theories.

One student wrote about child abuse, and whether people should be able to use their own abuse as a child as an "excuse" for future behavior. This student, after significant reflection, disagreed with the idea that our past can absolve us from responsibility for our own choices, writing: "Anyone can change his or her life around. Overall this was a unit that was appealing to me because it showed me that everyone has been through things and it depends on you to make the future what you want it to be."

As a final activity in this unit, Block created a partnership with the Leah Stein Dance Company, a local company that specializes in improvisational and site-based movement. The company is perhaps best known for its series of performances at the Eastern State Penitentiary, titled *Gate*, which sought to explore what it was like for prisoners to live and try to interact in an extremely dark, narrow, confining, and controlled space. Students worked with Stein over a period of months, culminating in a "Hidden City Festival," where students identified and performed in sites across the city to publicly explore the relationship between space, body, thoughts, touching, control, movement, freedom, and human emotions.

In their journals, many students noted that initially they were very uncomfortable with the assignment because they didn't know much about dance as a medium of expression, and they were not sure how to work together in their small groups, or to approach what was unique about the "space/site" they had chosen to explore. In the end, however, student reflections suggest that it was a unique and memorable experience:

> Through this experience I think I took away a lot more than I thought I would. I thought it would be just a stupid dancing thing where we go outside for a week and not learn anything. But I really feel like I have learned a lot about myself, my environment, and my friends. I now see my group members in a different way. They really impressed me with their really creative ideas. They were really able to see things around them that I would never see. In the same way I saw things myself that I would have never expected to see.

Likewise, Block sums up his view of the experience:

After reading *Night* and learning about the different experiences of prisoners in the US, students are very aware of different ways to define freedom and they are on a deeper level, questioning what it means to be human. Learning and then participating in the process of creating site specific dance pieces, many students are pushing themselves and accessing undiscovered parts of themselves. Through the process students become much more connected to the environment, to their bodies, to creative expression that is rooted in a collaborative group process, to the adventure of creating performance work for a public audience, and in some ways, to their deeper shared humanity.

Example 2: No *Easy A's* in This Class: Remaining Authentic in an Oppressive Society

Another example that demonstrates the power of interdisciplinary learning at the SLA is a senior elective called Sexuality and Society in Literature, taught by English teacher Alexa Klein Dunn. In this class, students were asked to read Hawthorne's classic novel *The Scarlet Letter* (1850) in conjunction with studying two recent films about teenage sexuality, *Juno* (2007) and *Easy A* (2010).

The three narratives were chosen to reflect the values and social mores of different times and cultures. The inclusion of *The Scarlet Letter* underscores that classical content (often associated with cultural literacy and standards) need not be marginalized or ignored in a progressive, inquiry, project-based curriculum and pedagogy. According to Dunn: "I believe in examining classic literature to give some weight and history to the ideas we're currently grappling with. . . . Many folks roll their eyes at *The Scarlet Letter* and believe it to be dated. However, when paired with the film *Juno*, one can see that Hester Prynne and June MacGuff experience similar issues as they are scorned and judged in the communities based on their choices." Many of the goals for this unit were closely aligned with English standards in schools across the country. For example, Dunn designed the unit so that students would gain experience in conducting a close reading of a text; being able to speak about key information in the text; becoming stronger readers through keeping written logs and taking effective notes on presentations and being able to summarize their reading.

At the same time, Dunn wanted her students to understand literacy as something that went beyond such "skills." She hoped that by engaging in with a complicated "canonical" text and contemporary films, students would be able to:

- see parallels between old and new stories based on similar themes
- decode text/film for plot lines, literary elements, subtext, and theme
- compare and contrast different media
- gain cultural literacy in both the past and the present

Students were given open-ended assignments, such as speculating about a character's motivation or what a character might have done differently. Indeed, because the story of *The Scarlet Letter* is centered on issues of acceptable sexual expression, gender roles and women's rights, and stereotyping and ostracizing, students can make connections between the characters in the story and their own experiences or similar issues in contemporary American culture.

For this very reason, it seemed natural to Dunn to pair *The Scarlet Letter* with contemporary films that address equally compelling issues about sexual freedom and expression. *Juno* explores teenage pregnancy and adoption, while *Easy A* is the story of a girl who gains popularity as she becomes known throughout her school for being "easy," perpetuating the myth that she allows her male classmates to lose their virginity to her. Over time, this aspect of her identity becomes all-consuming.

Students themselves crafted the questions that they wanted to explore throughout the unit, questions that shaped their thinking in a broader sense about the individual and society:

- How has society been influenced or perhaps even contradicted by the portrayal of love and sexuality in literature and media?
- How can we know when we've found love when society, media, and literature provide misleading information?
- How does society shape a person's sexual identity?
- How does one's nature conflict/reconcile with established societal laws/moral values/ideals? What is the interplay between the public and the private self?
- How does one remain authentic in a repressive society?

Instead of a traditional book report or written narrative reflecting on the relevance of the novel in contemporary times, students in Dunn's class were asked to "craft a creative piece that represents a theme or set of themes" from the three assigned stories, as well as to write a formal self-reflection about the purpose and process of doing this assignment.

Dunn gave students some ideas for the creative piece, although they were in no way limited to these suggestions. These included: a video montage to music; a monologue or dialogue; a collage or sculpture; a painting, drawing, or etching; a series of photographs; a choreographed dance; a podcast or radio play; a short story or long poem; a song with original lyrics; or a blog linking the three texts.

In a written reflection, Dunn asked students to create a comprehensive essay explaining their project, including the following directives: (1) A clear explanation of what your creative piece is about, what it represents, and how you attempted to get the point across. (2) How you went about crafting your piece. What was the process like? Did you encounter any problems/issues as you went along? (3) What are the aspects of the project you believe you did well? (4) What aspects of the project do you feel you could have done better? (5) If you could do it all over again, what would you do differently?

To help students get through *The Scarlet Letter*, which she acknowledges can be "a bit denser" than what students are used to, Dunn had them use "literature logs" to synthesize and process what they'd read and prepare for class discussion and activities. Students could choose from a variety of assignments, as long as they varied them. These included, among others:

- Create an interview with the author about a particular episode or chapter. What would you want to ask Nathaniel Hawthorne? How do you think he'd respond?
- Draw a picture of the reading (or a moment from the reading). Include a write-up as explanation of the piece. What is your drawing about? Why did you make the choices you made to create the scene in this way? What is portrayed in your scene and why is it significant?
- Write a reader response journal entry. . . .React to something in the selection that makes you uncomfortable, or something you take issue with.
- Make a newspaper story about one of the major events in the selection of reading. How would you as a journalist treat those events and how would the story be different than the author's interpretation?

Dunn hoped that by exploring these questions, students would gain a broader understanding of issues such as:

- How societal norms impact self-actualization.
- How true acceptance and understanding of self and others can take place regardless of society.
- How love is complicated and relationships survive based on a variety of factors.
- How there are many ways to express sexuality, and not all of them relate to love.

In keeping with the assignment to produce a creative piece that represents the themes of the three stories, many students innovated upon the teacher's suggestions and created photographic or video montages set to music, songs with original lyrics, and poems. Given the opportunity to come up with an entirely original idea, one student used his interest in fashion design and photography to create a series of T-shirts representing the identities of contemporary teen social outcasts. After silk-screening and producing the T-shirts, he had students volunteer to model them and photographed them in compelling scenes. The T-shirts included slogans such as: "I am a teenage mother"; "I am a homosexual"; "I am mentally challenged"; "I am a sex addict"; "I am a drug addict".

Reflecting on his project, the student writes:

> For this creative project, I decided to continue and expand upon [the course's themes of social outcasts] from a twenty-first-century perspective. At that moment I started to think deeply about what other outcasts there are in "the world of teens." I finally came up with the outcasting of teen motherhood, homosexuality, poverty, drug and sex addictions, sense of fashion, delinquency, and retardation. Those outcasts appeared to be the most significant of today, so it became the base of my creative project.
>
> From that point on, it became a matter of deciding which way would be best to represent these outcasts in a unique manner. . . . I created a combination of photography and a series of shirts as a final piece to display the outcasts of today. The line of clothing is entitled, "I Am An Outcast," each shirt design simply and boldly makes a statement for the public to see. The purpose for each shirt was to symbolize how we as a society judge each other for what appears in front of us before getting to know one another.
>
> With fashion, clothing does not speak alone without someone in it, so the second portion of the project became a photo shoot with various models to wear the clothes. In each picture the model stands alone to signify that they are separated from the rest of the world and are a unique person to themselves. . . .
> There has always been a passion for designing and fashion within me, but I've never been able to apply it in a meaningful way until now. . . . My next step to this project is to expand the clothing and deliver the message of social outcasting to more of the world.
>
> —Brett Chapman

The activities in this unit helped students to think more broadly about a range of issues related to identity, culture, and society, including:

* That societies differ from one another and change over time.
* That human relationships do not exist outside of social contexts, and it is important to look critically at the political and ideological systems that allow or constrict freedom and social justice.
* That it is important to understand what the author is trying to convey in a story, but it is also important to understand that there are many other ways to say the same thing or, perhaps, to present a different viewpoint.

Both of these examples of project-based learning exemplify a new kind of "risk-taking," as students come to understand that the study of history and literature does not have to be passive; students can learn from the past, while helping to create and rethink the future. And if at the end of all this teaching and learning students are still left with questions, so much the better.

QUESTIONS TO CONSIDER:

- How would you rewrite your school's mission in the form of questions? What questions would you choose, and why do you think they are significant questions to ask? If you have the opportunity, compare your questions to those of other staff or students. In what ways are they most strikingly similar or different?
- Are there certain questions that you would define as too risky in the current climate of educational reform? Why? How would you defend or address those risks?
- Does your school have common core values? *If so*, do you agree with them? What concerns do you have about them? What are some competing values? How would you change them? *If not*, what process would you suggest for selecting values, and what values would you advocate for? Do you think these values should ever change? Under what circumstances?
- Can you design a lesson plan based on a subject/topic you teach that both *begins* and *ends* in student inquiry? What does inquiry mean to you, and how can the inquiry process go beyond "right" and "wrong" answers? What other educational relationships can be defined by a process of inquiry besides those of a teacher asking questions of students?
- What would be the risks and possible benefits of letting students help guide the learning process and create their own unique end-product? What criteria would you have to use to evaluate the quality of student work, and how would you deal with the issue of subjectivity?
- How do students benefit from participating in a range of activities beyond reading, writing, and oral reports? Consider the role of technology, the arts and the many possible forms of creative expression, or the role of inservice learning.
- What role can student *and teacher* reflection play? What creative and meaningful ways can you think of to help students reflect upon their work in new ways? How can teachers work with students to enrich this process without dominating it?

NOTES

1. John Dewey, *Experience and Education* (New York: Free Press, 1997), 162.
2. See chapter 9 in A. Honigsfield and C. Cohen, *Breaking the Mold of School Instruction and Organization: Innovative and Successful Practices for the Twenty-First Century* (Lanham, MD: Rowman & Littlefield, 2010).

3. Hirsch, E.D. 1988. Cultural Literacy: What Every American Needs to Know. New York: Vintage Books.

4. *New York Times*, May 14, 1985.

Chapter Three

Courageous Conversations: Teaching, Cultural Identity, and Risk

The Folk Arts Cultural Treasures School (FACTS)

At FACTS we take a risk every time we involve students in something that is not going to be on the test. Academic excellence is the foundation, but it is not enough. At FACTS we believe that artistic pursuits, challenging questions and active involvement in the community prepare students for life outside of school.
—FACTS Principal Susan Stengel

We decided that if we were going to build a school it had to be a school that was consciously a school for democracy, a school for self-governance, a school for the creation of community.
—FACTS Founding Principal Deborah Wei

The Folk Arts Cultural Treasures School (FACTS) is a small K–8 charter school in Philadelphia's Chinatown that emerged from a ten-year struggle by parents and a community organization called Asian Americans United (AAU) to bring the first public school into the community. Seventy percent of the students are Asian (representing Chinese, Indonesian, Vietnamese, Cambodian, and Lao communities, among others); 20 percent are African American; and 10 percent are of African, Latino, mixed race, or European heritage. One-fourth are enrolled in the school's English Language Learner Program.

The FACTS embraces risk by approaching the education of minority and immigrant students from a resiliency model rather than deficit model. This means that the experiences, knowledge, wisdom, languages, opinions, ethics, and cultural values that students bring with them to school become a valued part of the curriculum, woven into all learning. The school does not seek to assimilate minority students into a superior "majority" culture, or, conversely, to position them as the "other." In this model, knowledge is not a commodity of preordained importance; instead, it must be understood within a specific context and point of view. The school embraces what could be called an intersectional approach to culture, which says that each of us belongs to many different identity groups and that these identities are not static.

FACTS AT A GLANCE

- Emphasis on cultural diversity, expression, and preservation throughout the curriculum.
- Creation of interdisciplinary folk arts standards for learning that guide the whole school's curriculum and pedagogy.
- Thematic/collaborative/experiential/project-based learning.
- Focus on intersectionality (not reducing people to stereotypical categories, and understanding that definitions of "us" and "them" are constructed, contextual, interactional, and fluid).
- Collaborative teaching, folk art residencies, learning from community members, and engagement with community-based elders and activists.
- Approaching students from nondominant cultures using a strength-based model, where bilingualism is nurtured and valued, rather than deficit or assimilation model.
- Mission to help students gain skills and confidence to participate in democracy and actively promote social justice, starting with their own communities.
- Emphasis on critically exploring multiple points of view, as well as comparing and deconstructing different sources of knowledge.
- Demographics: 70 percent Asian, 20 percent African American, and 10 percent multiracial, Hispanic, and white. Eighty-six percent of students qualify for free and reduced lunch. Twenty-five percent receive ESL services and 15 percent have Individualized Education Plans (IEP).

FOUNDING FACTS

In fifteen minutes, "Nine founders went to the School Reform Commission to get permission to found FACTS" became "A stampede of thinkers and visionaries stalked the Gods of wealth and decision to mercifully grant them permission to shutter the earth's core and unleash a temple of light."

This whole-class writing assignment was part of an exercise in Steven Coyle's eighth-grade history course; its ultimate intent was to help students learn more about Ancient Greece. On this day, they were learning about epic poetry. Coyle and a fellow teacher, Lucinda, worked as a team, beginning the lesson by asking students to volunteer to read parts of Homer's *Odyssey* out loud, in a dramatic fashion. Although the language was unfamiliar to many students, they worked together to bring Homer's poem to life:

> "Strangers," he said, "who are you? And where from?
> What brings you here by seaways—a fair traffic?
> Or are you wandering rogues, who cast your lives
> Like dice, and ravage other folk by sea?"
>
> We all felt pressure on our hearts, in dread
> of that deep rumble and that mighty man.
> But all the same I spoke up in reply:
>
> "We are from Troy, Achaeans, blown off course
> By shifting gales on the Great South Sea
> Homeward bound, but taking routes and ways
> Uncommon; so the will of Zeus would have it."

After thanking the volunteers, Teacher Lucinda explained to class that the Ancient Greeks didn't write down a lot of their narratives and history; instead they told stories out loud and created epic poems that were meant to be memorized and recited over and over. She then posed the question: "Why are epic poems so dramatic?" A student responded: "If it's boring, no one will remember it. If you want it to be passed down, it has to be exciting." Another student chimed in: "The dramatic language helps listeners really understand the feelings behind the words."

The teacher then asked: "What words and phrases tell you this is an epic poem?" Students respond that words like *ravage* are much more dramatic than *damage*, and the phrase *pressure on the heart* is much more evocative than just saying *shock* or *fear*.

By reciting and deconstructing the language and imagery that made Homer's poem "epic," then creating (as a group) their own "epic" version of a contemporary event (the founding of their own school), in a little over an hour the students learned about the history and culture of Ancient Greece, different forms of writing and narrative, new vocabulary words, and different ways of constructing history and describing historic events, such as oral history and dramatic reenactment. Students also explored differences in perspective and point of view, while engaging in collaborative writing, staged reading and storytelling, and a lot more.

Although this kind of interactive, creative learning was typical of any day at the FACTS, it is worth noting that this lesson took place on a very special day: Founders Day. Every year on March 9, the FACTS brings together students, teachers, families, founders, activists, and community members to celebrate and remember how and why the FACTS came to be. In particular, students reflect upon the founders' deep commitment to "reenvision what education could be and for, and also how an often marginalized community came together to organize, build and win support for this vision."[1] Founders Day shares the message that ordinary people working collectively can make change, that folk traditions like an annual celebration and origin narratives have relevance in our lives, and that we all have a role to play in creating the future we need and want.

Founded by Asian Americans United and the Philadelphia Folklore Project (PFP),[2] the FACTS was designed as "an alternative model to the development and gentrification" that had come to define Chinatown. According to Helen Gym at AAU: "Many of the founders were teachers or former teachers, as well as community advocates. They had long believed that schools could and should be community anchors." Gym went on to publicly raise the question: "Is there a different way to develop the community besides property value and real estate? Can a public school revitalize a community?" FACTS founding principal Deborah Wei said: "We needed to build a school that was consciously anti-individualist, antiracist, anti-isolationist, and anti-materialist. We wanted the school to be a place where children can claim a sense of community."

Each year on Founders Day, FACTS students—now drawn from neighborhoods all over the city—proudly walk around the school in bright red FACTS T-shirts that say, "I am a cultural treasure." What are cultural treasures? According to FACTS founders: "They are priceless. They are special. They hold our memories. They are dear to us. They are about more than a single person's experience." The very concept behind the FACTS was to open a school where formal and informal education, culture and community building, and globalism and social activism could all happen together.

FACTS Founders Day addresses many of these ideas, including:

What is Founders Day?

- Founders are people who find something—people who start something.
- At the FACTS, we are all finders. We are all founders.
- We are ordinary people: grown-ups and young people.
- We are making this school, all of us together, every day.
- We are people from many backgrounds and cultures.
- We are all working toward something, with justice and hope in our hearts. . . .

- We had to work hard (to struggle) for the rights to open the FACTS.
- It took a long time. It wasn't easy.
- Today is a day to remember how good it is to work together with other people for a dream of justice.

Why would we want to open our own school?

- Sometimes we see things that aren't fair or that make us sad or angry.
- And we want to change things.
- We wanted a school that put kids first, that respected culture, family, community, and art.

You are now also the ones making our new school.

- We are making a brand new school together now.

As the questions and statements above suggest, one of the key purposes of Founders Day is to help students at the FACTS understand that "founders" are more than just the individuals whose names make the history books. This does not mean that one person cannot have great influence or make a difference on his or her own, but even the most charismatic leaders depend on the input and support of so-called "ordinary people" to make their dreams come true.

> I want children to know that the school was not built quickly or easily. . . . I want children to know that many people with many skills contributed to this project, that it wasn't built or granted by people with titles and important positions.
> —FACTS founder Helen Gym

> There are Founders Days when you realize that the way sometimes history gets told is about heroes and big things that make you feel like you alone can't do anything to make a difference. There were the Founders days when you realize that if history is always told that way, people might never know how they can change the world.
> —Founder and first principal of the FACTS Deborah Wei

Throughout Founders Day, and year after year, students also come to realize that founding narratives are continually being revisited and expanded, *a process in which students themselves can have a role and become invested.* In other words, students come to better understand that *founding* something—be it an entire nation or a single school—is a long and enduring process rather than a single idea or event. They are asked to consider the questions: *What will you remember about this year? How are you helping to start this school, in a special way? What is your special contribution?* According to PFP director Debora Kodish: "Students are encouraged to see themselves as actors in history and as capable of making change that matters."

Founders Day thus helps students think more critically about and deconstruct all "foundation narratives," such as the different stories of how America was founded, or "discovered," by Columbus. Founders Day is an opportunity for students to talk about the ways that we name, share, frame, and document history, as well as how we teach about different histories in our schools. Students are also engaged in the process of storytelling and thinking about how they can be active in making our own histories.[3]

One year, students attending Founders Day listened to tapes and read transcripts of the arguments presented to the School Reform Commission (SRC) in favor of opening the FACTS. Students then reenacted the hearing process, playing different roles: commissioners, school district representatives, politicians, teachers, parents, community leaders. Some students played advocates for the FACTS, but others took on the role of those who questioned the need for it. As one of the founding members explained, through this process students learn what it feels like to "stand up and assume a risk," to "rely on others" while "speaking passionately for justice and change."

Recently, on March 9, 2011, students participated in an interactive performance with FACTS teachers reenacting events that led up to the school being granted its charter. Interspersed with dramatic episodes, were students reciting relevant parts of the FACTS pledge, a shared commitment that guides the school community day in and out.

FACTS PLEDGE: *We care for one another and learn together.*
There is no limit to what we can learn.
Our families and our elders know important things and we take time to learn from them.
We learn to help ourselves and our community.
We learn to be strong and act with courage.
All people have a right to use their own languages and honor their own cultures.
Creative expression is part of our lives and part of our school.
We work to build a fair and peaceful world.
The earth is our home and we must take care of it.

By orally weaving the pledge into the founders' stories, students come to understand that these sentiments are not purely rhetorical, nor are they meant to serve primarily as a basis for rules and control. For example, students recite, "We learn to be strong and act with courage," while teachers are telling the story of the founders' initial rejection by the School Reform Commission. Students recite, "Our families and elders know important things and we take the time to learn from them," while actors are telling individual stories of different people's role in helping to organize the FACTS, what this experience meant, and how participation changed conditions for an entire community.

WHY FOLK ARTS?

FACTS founding principal Debbie Wei says that the theme of "folk arts" was chosen to anchor the school because "folk arts challenge the notion that knowledge is a commodity—a thing you do to get a grade or get a job." Folk arts emphasize the many ways that knowledge is produced and shared besides textbooks, lectures, computers, and television, and the fact that "art" is a part of how we envision and recreate culture. Unfortunately, many students' knowledge of the folk arts come primarily from attending festivals, special assemblies, or going to museums—a pedagogy that does not engage students in doing folk arts or allowing them to experience the folk arts as they occur naturally within their genuine community contexts.

In contrast to notions of art as something that is the sole province of extraordinary or inherently talented individuals, the folk arts emphasize the fact that everybody can make art—which is not to say that the folk arts are easy or that they do not demand patience and devotion. While many folk artists are, in fact, extraordinary and inherently talented individuals at their particular artistic medium, the folk arts place an emphasis on active doing and making, broadening the definition of arts to include the skills and knowledge that are "central to living cultural traditions" in communities. Calling such traditions "folk" is a way of underscoring that communities are collectively built and thrive on shared ideas, visions, traditions, and the wisdom of their elders.

The folk arts theme helps students move past simplistic constructions of identity based only on their ethnicity or race; students begin to think about their own lives, and the way they view others in an *intersectional* framework. For example, from day one, students at the FACTS are asked to consider the many different kinds of groups they belong to (groups based on gender, age, neighborhood, classroom, and interests) and how these groups come to constitute communities (peer groups, friendship circles, teams). Students then consider differences *within* these categories of belonging—*beginner* vs. *expert, comfortable* vs. *uneasy, closeness* vs. *distance*—and, ultimately, how the categories of "us" and "them" are constructed and reconstructed in different historic and political contexts, and through different ideologies and communications mediums.

A folk arts committee developed in partnership with the school, Asian Americans United, and the Philadelphia Folklore Project created the following four folk arts standards to guide their vision of the entire school:[6]

- Understanding who I am and who is around me.
- Learning how I can explore folk arts and folklife, and sharing what I know.
- Recognizing folk arts as an active force in society and in the world around us.
- Becoming an active, respectful culture maker.

Using these standards to guide them, students are asked not only to name the different cultures with which they identify themselves, but also how these differences are constructed and transformed within the politics of colonialism, acculturation, and assimilation. They consider the ways that folklife traditions are practiced and perceived, such as: *making invisible, discounting, shallow mimicry, appreciation, affirming,* and *critically honoring.*

Students also learn about the range of methodologies for studying and understanding different cultural practices, including opportunities to engage in *action research, collecting oral histories, doing ethnography, debating, designing scientific experiments,* and *conducting community surveys.*

The standards also emphasize the idea that knowledge is not static and that it is important to consider such questions as: *Who is creating the message? What is its purpose? How is it transmitted?* and *What power and resources lie behind it?* Such questions lead students to more complex explorations of how "particular traditions support or hurt the practice of equity, empathy or peace."

Another central part of the FACTS design is offering students opportunities to work closely with community folk artists, in the form of residencies, which often last several weeks or even months. The FACTS has had resident folk artists practicing and teaching the Chinese art of Hung Gar Kung Fu and lion dance, Liberian song, African American storytelling, Tibetan sand mandalas, and Cambodian costume-and mask-making. The goal is not only to learn the art form itself, but also to think about the life stories and motivations of individual artists. To do this, they must grapple with critical questions, such as:

- Where were important turning points, challenges, and opportunities?
- Are there parts of their stories that are important to you, that interest you, or that remind you of something?
- What other skills do they have besides the art for which they are known?
- What were important achievements in their lives?
- What are they proud of? (How do you know? How can you tell?)

- Are these common things to be counted as achievements? (Why or why not, do you think?)
- Compare the lives of two artists. How are they the same and how are they different?
- What else do you want to know/wish you knew about these artists?
- Why do these artists do this art form?
- What rewards do they get?

Students are encouraged not only to learn about different folk arts, but to "pass on or act" on the knowledge they gain.

MANY POINTS OF VIEW DAY

Another day observed at the FACTS occurs every year on October 12—a day when most public- and private-school students have the day off. It is officially celebrated in the United States as Columbus Day, or the day Christopher Columbus "discovered" America. At the FACTS, they call it Many Points of View Day. Though it is still a special day, school is open and full attendance is expected.

The day begins with the entire student body, staff, and visitors (parents, community members) gathering in the largest room in the school. Like many events at the FACTS, the day begins in song. The song they sing, taken from the publication *Rethinking Columbus*, reflects the rest of the day's activities in that it does not seek to vilify Columbus. The goal of the song—which is even more apparent in the additional verse added by the FACTS founding principal—is to help students think more critically about how history is framed and constructed from different perspectives and for different purposes:

1492, by Nancy Schimmel (final verse by Deborah Wei) [7]

In fourteen hundred and ninety-two
Columbus sailed the ocean blue
It was a courageous thing to do
But someone was already here.

Columbus knew that the world was round,
So he looked to the east, while Westward bound,
But he didn't find what he thought he found,
And someone was already here.

Refrain

The Inuit and Cherokee, the Aztec and Menominee
Onondaga and the Cree (clap clap);
Columbus sailed across the sea,
But someone was already here.

It isn't like it was empty space,
The Caribs met him face to face.
Could anyone discover a place,
When someone was already here?

Refrain

So tell me, who discovered what?
He though he was in a different spot.
Columbus was lost, the Caribs were not
They were already here.

Refrain

And it's up to me and you,
To understand different points of view
To have our own opinions too,
That's what we want to do here.

Refrain

After the song, and some community-building games and interactive sto-rytelling, the day then proceeds with a combination of regular classes and special activities. The day is designed to engage students in age-appropriate discussions about culture, colonialism, globalization, industrialization, historical narrative, and representation. Two innovative examples, designed for children of different age groups, show how teachers and students in FACTS classrooms are embracing risk.

Example 1: If We Don't Always Know for Sure, Why Do We Study It at All?

In his eighth-grade history class, Steve Coyle uses a wide variety of primary and secondary source materials, including textbooks, memoirs, speeches, debate transcripts, slave narratives, oral histories, songs, photographs, and films. When they read about history from any source, Coyle asks his students to consider a big question: how do we know our perception of history is accurate? His students must read the texts not only for what they say, but also for what they don't say: *What information do you think is left out of this passage? What groups of people seem NOT to be mentioned?*

Coyle wants students to understand that "textbooks are often written with political motivations in mind" and to become familiar with vocabulary words like *inference, perception*, and *ignorance*. In line with the FACTS's larger goals of incorporating folk arts into the standard curriculum, Coyle also wants students to decode the ways history is conveyed in pictures, songs, rhymes, traditions, customs, and movement, as well as in words.

On the first day of class in September, for example, Coyle puts up two pictures—one of an Asian immigrant family and the other of a wealthy African American family. He tells his students to take one minute to write down anything that comes to their minds when looking at the photos. Then he asks:

- Who do you think these families are? When do you think these photos were taken?
- What can we tell about them? How do you think they feel about themselves? How do they survive? Can you tell by looking at a picture?
- What do you notice the most?

Students' responses range significantly in observation, detail, and supposition. For example: "I think they are a Chinese family"; "I think they are a rich family because they are wearing white clothes"; "They look like they lived a long time ago"; "I can tell they're a family because they look alike"; "They look unhappy because they are not smiling"; "They are not from China because they're wearing 'like' suits (Western clothing) that they wear in America, not traditional clothing."

These questions led to Coyle's big build-up: "If these photos don't tell the whole story and can even deceive us about their identities, why would we use them as a source?" This is a risky question. Indeed, as Patricia Hill Collins suggests, it can be scary for young children to "confront the idea that truth and lies are not fixed ideas, and so-called facts reflect the point of view of whoever has the power to define it." Yet, as Collins also notes, this same process can be "freeing," as students begin to "practice thinking about themselves as part of this process of sorting ideas into categories" and recognizing that they can "disrupt the everyday assumptions that uphold disciplinary power."[8]

Likewise, when Coyle's students gather together on Many Points of View Day, they get a two-sided handout to read quietly to themselves. One side is titled "Columbus' Story" and the other side is titled "The Taino Story." The two narratives present conflicting points of view about Columbus's actions, intent, and impact on native cultures.

For example, in "Columbus' Story," written entirely in the first person and focusing primarily on his own dreams, actions, and impressions, Columbus says:

"I dreamed of being a sailor. . . . Most people thought the ocean was too wide to cross. They said it cannot be done! And sailing west over the ocean would be expensive! I did not have enough money. . . . I went to see the King and Queen of Spain. At first they said no . . . , but I told them about my dreams of riches. Finally they said yes, they would help me. I promised to bring back many riches for the King and Queen. . . . After six months away, I returned to Spain. I brought some native people with me. I was welcomed as a great hero!! I was very happy."

In contrast, the Taino Story is written in a much more complicated narrative style, shifting between *I* and the plural forms of *we* and *my people*:

Once upon a time, I lived on an island called Hayti. . . . We were proud of our island. We built beautiful farms and villages. We had many plants and animals. There were many of us. We called ourselves Taino. One day, some of my people saw three boats far off in the ocean. . . . When the boats reached land, strange looking people got off. . . . Their leader was a man named Christopher Columbus. He put a cross and a flag down on our beach. Through his motions, we thought he said the land now belonged to him.

Though many schools critically explore the use of the word *discovery* to describe Columbus's encounter with America, a significant part of Columbus's story remains largely unknown. As students continue to read the Taino story, they learn significant details hidden behind Columbus's statement that he "brought" some native people with him upon returning to Spain:

After several months, Columbus returned to our island for a second visit. He brought hundreds of people on 17 boats. Before he left this time, he forced more than 500 of our people onto his boats. We later learned they were all taken to Spain and sold as slaves. Many died during the trip.

More facts about the brutal impact of Columbus's legacy on the Taino people are then revealed:

Columbus told our people to bring him gold. But it was so hard to find. If we did not bring him gold, his men cut off our hands. . . . Many of my people killed themselves. After 2 years, more than half of my people died.

As FACTS students read these two narratives, they make notes on another handout, this one titled *Christopher Columbus: Hero or Villain?* Students chart in one column the things they already knew or thought about Columbus and, in another, what they learned from reading the Taino story. Similarly, in a related assignment students are given an organizer that helps them chart the following categories of information: (1) facts; (2) information we believe to be true based on evidence; and (3) information that is disputed by a second source or is present in only one source.

This process lets students become historians themselves, as they sort out opinion from fact, and, more importantly, consider how opinion and fact are often conflated and distorted by power relationships. According to Coyle:

> It teaches skill as well as content. Students must read, analyze, and compare multiple perspectives that tell the story of the same historical event or sequence. It teaches students to pay attention to WHO wrote the story they are reading and what might be their perspective. It teaches students to consider the parties in the story as all having a side. In other words, the historical event wasn't just about Columbus, and the others involved were just there to "fill in details of the story."

Coyle also asks his students to brainstorm what they know about Columbus in the context of their own lives. One student calls out, "In Philadelphia we used to have something called Delaware Avenue, but the name has been changed to Columbus Boulevard." Coyle follows up with a question: "What ethnic groups live near Columbus Boulevard, and do you think this had any impact on the fact that the street was renamed?" The students quickly catch on that this neighborhood is largely made up of immigrants from Italy, Columbus's birthplace.

The larger purpose of this activity, as with all assignments in Coyle's class, is to help students develop their critical thinking skills by connecting past events to current conditions, and analyzing the role that ordinary citizens and policy leaders play in shaping each era of American history. According to Coyle, in a school with many minority and immigrant students, teaching Columbus in this way can be risky:

> Most students are at the point in life when they are trying to find out who they are. It is an easy question to answer if you get the traditional American training. You can answer: "I am American. I live in a country discovered by Christopher Columbus in 1492, and since then, we have done nothing but good things. We created democracy, we freed slaves, we stopped Hitler, we let everyone get rich if they want, and we give food to Africa. We do good things, and since *I* am an American, I *must* be good, strong, brave, and merciful, too."
>
> But . . . having students learn of Columbus as a historian would—reading multiple sources that spill little secrets like he MAY have caused the genocide of 300,000 Tainos—changes all of this. Now they learn to think critically about what they are reading and to question *unquestionable* sources, i.e., a textbook, a teacher, a movie, a song, a national anthem, a pledge, a flag, and a story about a guy, his vision, and his three ships—the Niña, the Pinta, and the Santa Maria.
>
> The risk? A student must come up with their own answer to the question, "Who am I?" And the first answer might be not be "I am an American," and that scares a lot of people.

In Coyle's class, students know both that they are Americans and that they also have to live with and make sense of labels such as *citizen, naturalized, resident*, or *other*. Yet according to Coyle, this risk comes with a reward: it leads students to think about "what it *really* means to be an American," including "which heroes and ideas are worthy of our reverence" and how students themselves can "continue those legacies." In Coyle's classroom, the goal of each lesson is to investigate historical acts *as a way of prompting students to be active themselves in shaping the future*. As one of Coyle's favorite historians, Howard Zinn, has argued, part of the purpose of going into history is to come out of it.

Coyle seeks to help his students understand how past events that appear on the surface to be very specific in nature often have ongoing and far-reaching effects on whole social systems. For example, when studying the causes of the Civil War, Coyle's students read a mini-play in class about the Dred Scott decision. In addition to analyzing the decision's impact on slavery, Coyle asks his students to think about its impact on state rights. This, in turn, generated a student-centered discussion about other, more contemporary state-based laws, such as those related to same-sex marriage, capital punishment, and legalization of marijuana.

Going one step further, students were asked to take the historical arguments they identified in the Dred Scott decision and use them to formulate a position on questions such as:

• If you get married in Massachusetts (same sex) and move to a state that doesn't have it [same-sex marriage], should the new state recognize your marriage and give you all legal benefits, such as taxes [or] not testifying against your spouse?
• If you have a license for marijuana in one state and drive to another that hasn't decriminalized it yet, are you breaking the law?
• Should Massachusetts, a state that does not have the death penalty, extradite a fugitive to a death penalty state, even if the fugitive had established residency in Massachusetts before the crime was allegedly committed?

Eventually, discussions about states' rights and the American legal system lead Coyle's students into a broader conversation about American citizenship and identity. "It doesn't matter what country's history you are studying in class," he says. "Your students generally want to learn why people did things, what people do things, and are they anything like these people that they are studying?"

Coyle's approach to teaching history from multiple perspectives, and as a narrative that is open to interpretation and revision, is reflected on the tests he gives. At the end of the lesson on Dred Scott, for example, Coyle created a test that begins with straightforward multiple-choice questions such as "How did John Brown attempt to abolish slavery?" before moving on to short-answer questions such as "What were the economic differences between the North and South before the Civil War?"

Students are then asked to reread a passage from the Dred Scott play and answer much more complex, open-ended questions, such as:

- David Hall is talking about the laws of more than one state in this passage. Why? Why is *this* his argument? (Try to mention your knowledge of the Constitution in your answer); and
- Think of an example of a modern-day "state-to-state" issue. We have mentioned many in class that have caused conflict between two state laws. Describe the conflict, what both sides want/claim and any other information that you know about it.

The test requires students to use increasingly complex analytical and reasoning skills. In one section, for example, students are asked to review and analyze a political cartoon from the era portraying a tug of war between the Union (represented as a pole with the U.S. flag on top, and South Carolina (represented in the form of a Donkey). The caption reads: *Southern, Ass-stock-crazy*.

Eventually, in the final leg of the test, Coyle asks his middle-school students to demonstrate an ability to read, analyze, and write about primary source documents much like college-educated adult historians:

> *Section V Essay:* Reread the following excerpt that we read and analyzed in class surrounding a *Fourth of July* celebration. Write a two- to three-paragraph essay that identifies the *speaker*, his *purpose*, his *tone*, and his *message*. You should make sure to mention his language and vocabulary choices (we discussed in class) and their meaning.

> Excerpt: *"At a time like this, scorching irony, not convincing argument, is needed. O! had I the ability, and could reach the nation's ear, I would, to-day, pour out a fiery stream of biting ridicule, blasting reproach, withering sarcasm, and stern rebuke. For it is not light that is needed, but fire; it is not the gentle shower, but thunder. We need the storm, the whirlwind, and the earthquake. The feeling of the nation must be quickened; the conscience of the nation must be roused; the propriety of the nation must be startled; the hypocrisy of the nation must be exposed; and its crimes against God and man must be proclaimed and denounced."*

Example 2: Experiencing Colonialism: When Play-Doh Isn't Just for Playing.

With younger children, the teachers at the FACTS take a different approach toward the same goal of having them think more critically about different points of view. The fourth- and fifth-graders gather together on Multiple Points of View Day to take part in a village-building exercise that helps them experience the impact of colonialism and industrialization.

Students are divided into groups, given supplies of multicolored Play-Doh, and instructed to use the modeling compound to create their own villages on paper mats set out before them. They must sit on the floor and work in silence. The teachers' reasons behind asking for silence include: (1) setting a mood that makes it clear that this is a learning activity as opposed to an extra recess period (especially since the medium used is Play-Doh instead of paper and pencils), and (2) making sure that everyone can hear what the teachers are saying as they roam the crowded room and visit the groups. But silence also replicates the way that many individuals and communities have been forced to industrialize in a competitive rather than cooperative fashion, without empathy, sharing ideas and looking for consensus.

The students begin using their Play-Doh to build houses, trees, benches, animals, rivers, and plants, among other things. As they do, the teachers walk around the room, tower over a particular village and make comments such as: "I love that bush. You did a really great job! I'm going to take that bush and add it to the teachers' village over here." With that, the teachers, in the guise of complimenting the children, take away their precious resources; the children have to rebuild or do without.

This goes on for more than half an hour. At the same time, the teachers also randomly point to students, remove them from their groups, and tell them to do one of two things: (1) sit quietly against the wall as if they were in trouble, but for no identifiable reason; or (2) come to the teachers' table and use the items the teachers have collected to help build the teachers' village. Though the students grow increasingly frustrated and perplexed, most do not protest or ask the teachers to explain their actions. The students who were pulled out of their groups to sit by the wall are visibly upset during the activity, although only one or two question the teacher: "What did I do wrong?" "Was I talking . . . is that why you called me out?"

At the end of the activity, the teachers say, in a serious tone of voice: "Well, you did a good job with your individual villages. But looking around, you have to admit that our village is the best." The students see a bunch of villages on paper mats on the floor that have been ravaged. Then they see the teacher's village, surrounded by the specially designated student helpers, who seem to be happy that they were chosen but uncomfortable with what they have been asked to do. The teacher's village is overflowing with resources that have been appropriated from the student's villages.

The discussion begins. The teachers ask the students: How did your feelings change from the beginning of the activity to the end? Is power good or bad? What is empathy? What is *point of view,* and what factors influence one's point of view? As a result of this activity, what is your perspective on the Native Americans? Columbus? Explorers?

Most of the students agree that they were very eager at first, primarily because of the opportunity to work with Play-Doh. Quite a few say that it is exciting to be asked to use Play-Doh instead of paper and pencils or more traditional artistic materials like paints and markers. They felt that this was special, and they were enthusiastic to get started. But for many students, that enthusiasm soon turned to confusion, as they watched their work—or that of their peers—taken away and added to the teachers' table.

Several express their feelings by saying things like, "I didn't understand why the teachers were doing that" and "I started to get a little mad" and even "It made me sad to leave my group." On the other hand, students who were told to go to the teachers' village and to "work faster" to build pieces for the teachers comment that they didn't necessarily feel angry or sad. Instead, they were focused on doing the best work that they could (after all, they were now building for the TEACHERS' village!); initially, it seemed like an honor to be chosen to work for the teachers. As time went on, however, these same students began to feel uncomfortable. Periodically stealing glances back to their own group, they began to worry about the growing disintegration of their original villages. "I was happy and not happy," said one student.

At the end of the activity, a handful of students remain angry, even though the teachers explain that they *purposely* behaved in that manner to teach about power and point of view during colonialism. A few students ask, "Why couldn't you think of another way to teach this lesson?" though most of them audibly express an "aha" moment when they realize what was going on. On the written evaluation forms that the students are asked to complete, many say how much they didn't like the feeling of being overpowered by the teachers, even more than they might have expected.

This activity followed a morning session in which students learned about Columbus and his treatment of the natives in the more traditional manner of lecture and discussion. Students thought Columbus' behavior was "unfair" to the Native Americans, but many said that they "didn't really know HOW unfair" until they participated in the afternoon activity. Some said that they "felt sorry" for the natives and were "mad" at Columbus. In this way, students began to think more deeply about the role of empathy in the construction and understanding of history.

One of the teachers who created the activity, Katherine Brody, reflected on its value:

> In my classroom we had had some previous discussions about empathy and point of view, but I believe that this exercise clearly reinforced the students' understanding of these concepts. Some students concluded that it is "easier" to show empathy when you have had the same experiences and that understanding one's point of view is "harder" when you haven't.
>
> Whenever possible we try to provide students with opportunities to truly experience the concept we're trying to teach—it is much more powerful than just talking about it. Instead of asking students to *imagine* how Natives might have felt, living that experience—even to a smaller degree—is so much more meaningful.

The village activity is a wonderful example of teaching and learning that *embraces risk.* But teachers must be prepared to explain themselves and make clear connections to the content being covered, as well as to support and even comfort students who will have responses ranging from "aha" moments to anger and confusion. As in chapter 2, when SLA teacher Joshua Block had his students simulate what it's like to be crowded together and imprisoned, teachers must be prepared for highly emotional responses when they attempt to get students to experience a concept rather than simply be able to define or intellectually explain it.

A few months after the exercise, Brody says:

> Any hands-on activity is risky . . . even though student motivation and engagement increase (hooray!), because of the excitement "new" materials often generate, so can the noise level. It is easy for teachers—particularly those who are accustomed to relying primarily on pencil and paper tasks—to feel a loss of control when incorporating different media in lessons.
>
> It was also risky to co-teach this activity. There were four to five teachers all working together to lead the activity. We had to deal with elements of trust and responsibility, to make sure we had clarity about our objectives. Also, we had no written plan or script. Based on our previous relationships and collaborations with each other, we knew that we could trust each other to deliver a cohesive presentation.
>
> And, even though we met in one of our school's largest open spaces, it was still a gamble to have one hundred students all in one room! It was also risky to group students from four different classes together, knowing that many did not know each other's names and had not worked collaboratively before.
>
> Most of all, the activity itself was risky in that some students may have had a hard time understanding the "pretend" nature of the activity. Our experience from a simulation the year before alerted us to this possibility, however, and we were prepared for some negative reactions.

Brody's emphasis on the importance of "preparing" for negative reactions is a key part of understanding the concept of *embracing risk* in education. Teachers taking risks in the classroom, and encouraging students to do the same, almost ensures that there will be uncomfortable exchanges to contend with. But these moments of disagreement or uncertainty can be turned into something positive and productive by what those at the FACTS call *courageous conversations*.

Courageous Conversations (by Susan Stengel, principal of the FACTS)

FACTS takes time every year on professional development days for *courageous conversations*. These are two to four hour blocks of time when teachers and staff are required to think and talk about issues of race, culture, language, socioeconomics, or other factors that affect education. The topics for discussion are often difficult and often raise controversial points of view. The goal of these conversations is to make conscious the ways in which the attitudes, beliefs, and experiences that are a part of our own individual cultural identities manifest themselves in our teaching.

Sometimes, we schedule a specific activity. A few examples are listed below:

• We watched a segment of *Dateline NBC* regarding the Harvard Implicit Association Test, which is an online test that attempts to score attitudes and biases on race, skin hue, age, and other factors. We encouraged staff to take the test and held discussion afterward. Staff members were surprised and embarrassed to learn about some of their unconscious assumptions and the ways that they might unwittingly treat students differently. We all vowed to be more aware during daily classroom interactions.
• We viewed a few segments from a film about code-switching and then talked about what code-switching might mean to an Asian student who is just learning English or to an African American student who might notice the difference between the English she speaks at home and the English that is expected of her at school. The result of the conversation was a plan for introducing the concept of code-switching to our students and a set of guidelines for teachers concerning standards for spoken English at school.

Other times, courageous conversations are just that—a conversation. For example, we held a discussion *about* discussing the achievement gap, during which a significant portion of the staff said they were uncomfortable even saying the words *black* or *Asian*, not to mention discussing differences in achievement by race.

Courageous conversations may make people uncomfortable at first, but the hope is that respect, repetition, and frequency will create a safe space for important issues of culture, identity and educational equity to be made visible and actively addressed. Ultimately, we believe that students will benefit from this careful examination and that, as a staff, we will be drawn closer together in our common endeavor.

QUESTIONS TO CONSIDER:

- How does your school define what constitutes "the arts" and is there any discussion of the difference between mainstream arts and "folk arts"?
- Likewise, are certain forms of art more valued than others? If so, what characterizes these elevated art forms? Are they primarily centered on *individual* mastery or on ensemble work and community building?
- Are certain groups of children in your school more likely to be exposed to certain arts than others, and how varied are these exposures? If so, how would you define these groups, and why do you think this is the case?
- What does it mean to you to declare students themselves a "cultural treasure"?
- How does your school construct the boundaries and hierarchies involved in teaching and learning? What kinds of opportunities exist for students to work with community elders, artists, change agents, and coalition builders? What do you think students can get from observing and interacting with community members/elders that they may not get from the lecture format?
- Do the teachers and students in your school have structured opportunities to learn about (and actively research) the school's history and founding, as well as its original, evolving and present-day relationship to the surrounding community? Is this relationship even considered important in your school culture?
- What ideas do you have for helping students "experience" what you are trying to teach them (for example, the activity in which children experienced colonialism)? What are the potential benefits to this kind of pedagogy? What about the risks? Would it be different if students themselves were asked to design and lead these kinds of experiential activities?
- When you write tests at the end of a unit plan, do you consciously try to include a variety of different question-and-answer formats? What is the value of having multiple choice, short answer, cartoon or visual analysis, and essay writing all together in one test? Consider Coyle's test about the Civil War; would you use a similar format in your own tests?

- What kind of professional development opportunities are available to teachers at your school? How are these meetings organized and led? Are teachers intrinsically involved in the planning and setting the agenda? What kinds of issues are more or less commonly discussed?
- If your goal was to encourage *courageous conversations* among educators and/or students, what kinds of questions would you pose?
- How have your answers to the questions above changed from when you began teaching (for example, as a result of the test-heavy era of No Child Left Behind and Race to the Top)?

NOTES

1. Quote from Helen Gym and Allen Somekawa of Asian Americans United.

2. Both organizations are still very active in curriculum development, professional development, and student-enrichment activities at the FACTS.

3. For more information about how the FACTS got started, please refer to http://www.culturaltools.org/community/facts.html.

6. For more information about the creation of the school's Folk Arts Standards and "Resources for Folk Arts Education," see the website of the Philadelphia Folklore Project at www.folkloreproject.org.

7. N. Schimmel, Original Song in Rethinking Columbus, a special publication of the journal Rethinking Schools edited by Bill Bigelow and Bob Peterson. Song teprinted with the permission of the author. This song can be listened to on-line at http://www.sisterchoice.com/1492.mp3

8. Collins, P.H. (2010). Another Kind of Public Education: Race, Schools, the Media and Democratic Possibilities. Boston: Beacon Press

Chapter Four

When Superman Is Delayed: Social Justice, Student Activism, and Risk

Parkway NW School for Peace and Social Justice

We do not look at a "Peace School" as the absence of difference or change but as a place to become active and passionate. In order for our students to develop intellectual passions they need experiential tools which allow them to engage with difficult concepts. Funding for fieldtrips to museums, youth conferences, international experiences, art projects, and speakers facilitates the creation of these tools. Students take new experiences and use them every day when they encounter intolerance, violence and other detriments to peace.
—From the blog of the Parkway Northwest School for Peace and Justice

This chapter explores the Parkway Northwest School for Peace and Social Justice. Though it would be easy to assume from its name that the school embraces a particular ideological position, the school's founders had something broader and more innovative in mind. As the opening quote suggests, Parkway NW seeks to help students become more intellectually engaged by building an academic curriculum that is truly relevant to their lives. With a student population composed almost entirely of urban African Americans (most of them from low-income families), Parkway NW sought a new way to engage students who might otherwise have been "at-risk" for dropping out, feeling powerless, or being involved in violent conflicts.

Yet the model for Parkway NW stands in stark contrast to other well-known schools also seeking to serve disadvantaged students. There is no Superhero effort to "save" and "assimilate" minority students into a predefined majority "culture of success." Parkway NW School for Peace and

Social Justice embraces risk by helping students from dangerous and/or disadvantaged communities develop the skills to mediate conflict, while giving them opportunities to publicly challenge injustices in their own lives, and around the world. Though it is still considered a "college preparatory" high school, Parkway NW seeks to help students develop a deeper understanding of the origins and impact of issues such as racism, sexism, homophobia, and poverty.

In addition to creating a safe environment within the school for students to learn without fear, Parkway NW teaches students that they have the power, the initiative, and the obligation to help others in need. Service-learning is a significant part of the school's pedagogy. The school creates opportunities for students to work together to fundamentally change the systems that create such desolation in the first place. The curriculum is designed to teach students that all knowledge is political, along with the skills of critical literacy and engaged leadership.

PARKWAY NORTHWEST AT A GLANCE

- Explicit commitment to teaching student mediation and violence prevention, and exploring larger political issues around peace and social justice;
- Global curriculum with opportunities for students to learn from peers in other countries and cultures through technology and school trips;
- Emphasis on collaborative learning, including students' teaching and designing their own assessment tools;
- Centralized Student Development Center, a student-led group that organizes student activities such as protests, teach-ins, fundraisers, awareness campaigns, debates, festivals, and other community-based events;
- Demographics: 99 percent African American, 1 percent Latino, 10 percent special education, 61 percent reduced lunch.

THE LONG ROAD TO [A] PEACE [SCHOOL]

The physical journey from center city Philadelphia to the Parkway Northwest School for Peace and Social Justice is a long one, much like the conceptual journey the school itself went through when it changed from a small, traditional college-preparatory high school to a national model for peace and social justice education.

The number 23 bus takes over an hour to get to the school from Philadelphia's City Hall, passing through one economically depressed neighborhood after another. Blocks and blocks of houses, public institutions, and businesses are shuttered and abandoned. Many small businesses still have signs, but show no indication that they will open anytime soon. Empty lots, sometimes half a block long, are practically buried in trash.

At the same time, the bus will travel through the well-regarded campus of Temple University, past beautiful murals and brightly colored, painted, and mosaic sculptures, and the prestigious private school Germantown Friends. The journey down Philadelphia's historic Germantown Avenue will showcase a number of historic houses, museums, and sites, such as the Johnson House, an Underground Railroad site, and the Cliveden House, which was central to the 1777 Battle of Germantown in the Revolutionary War.

By the time you get off the bus at 7500 Germantown Avenue, you truly don't know what kind of school to expect. Indeed, Parkway NW is hard to find: the small, no-frills, three-story school building is almost fully eclipsed by the building in front of it; the entrance to the school is marked only by a small sign. The school itself is housed back from the street on a site known as the New Covenant Campus, a cluster of buildings that includes a Waldorf school and a historic church. Unlike the stereotypical urban public high school, Parkway NW sits on a serene, grassy green campus set with picnic tables, shady trees, and walking paths.

As in many urban public schools, when you walk into Parkway NW you are confronted with a security guard and metal detector. But the narrow hallways are filled with flyers for rallies and protests, volunteer activities, fundraisers, and other upcoming events. The walls are covered with photographs of students at sites throughout the community: marching, dancing, teaching, serving food, making and selling protest buttons and T-shirts. There is a plethora of student writing and artwork, ranging from drawings and poems on topics such as "What is Philadelphia?" to scathing commentaries on issues such as human trafficking and child abuse.

Parkway NW was not always designated a school for *peace and social justice*. Before it became a peace school, it was a traditional academic, multipurpose high school that was part of a district wide initiative to create smaller alternatives to Philadelphia's neighborhood high schools, which typically enrolled over three thousand students. The idea behind creating small schools was that more personal attention and interaction with teachers and counselors would not only improve student achievement, but also reduce troublesome dropout levels and discipline problems.

When then Superintendent Paul Vallas opened the region's first public military academy in the area, a group of concerned educators and community organizations—recognizing the high level of violence so many urban children must cope with daily—wanted to offer an alternative. Working closely with the American Friends Service Committee, Arcadia University, and Military Families Speak Out, a local nonprofit called Public Citizens for Children and Youth (PCCY) championed the idea for a "peace school" that would explicitly teach students about ways to mediate conflicts that did not include physical threats or violence. According to the school's mission statement, it sought to build a program to help students "learn to decrease violence, advance justice, work with people of different backgrounds, and help create a culture of peace."

Advocates, teachers, and administrators, however, wisely realized that it would take more than simply crafting a new mission statement to create a school for peace and social justice. According to Principal Ethyl McGee, who led the transition, within the course of one year the school changed its entire focus, organization, pedagogical practices, curriculum, and extracurricular offerings *without* substantially changing its leadership or teaching staff. Still a part of the school district of Philadelphia, the school still had to work with limited resources and make sure it complied with federal mandates, such as AYP.

Parkway NW thus created an advisory committee that included representatives from a wide array of activist and community-based organizations. Under the guidance of the advisory committee, the faculty worked with Educators for Social Responsibility and local nonprofits to engage in professional development and to create new courses, after-school programs, and other innovative learning opportunities. The school instituted in-service placements in the community, regular guest speakers known for their leadership and activism, monthly seminars on a variety of peace-related topics, social leadership classes, and a peer-mediation training program.

These experiences were all designed to "teach students to care about one another, to critically examine violence and social justice issues, and to foster skills and adopt actions that will help resolve social problems." For example, over four years, all students must donate a minimum of sixty hours of service and leadership to the local community in order to graduate. Students tap into their own passions and interests to choose where they want to concentrate their energies, including working to rebuild homes in economically depressed communities; working on election campaigns; volunteering at museums, historic sites, community centers, and cooperatives; reading to children at homeless shelters; working with the elderly; or promoting literacy at public libraries.

In addition, during their senior year all students design and implement a multidisciplinary project based on a real-world problem involving an existing community or social service agency. Recent student projects have included working with a local food co-op on the problem of minorities and obesity; working with the Philadelphia Streets Department to explore environmental racism and classism; and working with Town Watch Integrated Services and Good Sheppard Mediation Center to show how conflict-resolution and mediation skills can decrease crime in local communities. Students eventually present what they have learned to a panel of teachers and community mem-

bers, analyzing complex statistical data, exploring the impact of social policies and services, and giving their own concrete ideas for improving or
changing current conditions. Many students' ideas are put into practice by
city agencies.

All ninth-graders at Parkway NW also take part in extensive peer-mediation training led by a consultant from Educators for Social Responsibility
(ESR). Likewise, all ninth- and tenth-grade students must take a series of
social leadership classes, which include what the school calls "ethical fitness
training." This draws heavily on a program called Champions of Caring, a
character education and service-learning curriculum that invites students to
reflect on the challenges they and their contemporaries face, to better understand these challenges in historical and political context, and to develop
"strategies and skills that will help them confront those challenges."

In the social leadership classes, which they take *in addition* to their regular schedule of required college-prep subjects, students consider their own
personal styles of leadership, as well as how they define social justice and
actively contribute to creating a more socially just world. In the process,
students also learn techniques for anger management, active listening, disagreement, dialogue and debate, and critical inquiry, and they engage in
activities designed to help them more critically analyze the impact of contemporary media and public policies, both on popular culture and in their
own cultures and communities.

The school created its own Student Community Development Center
(SCDC), a *student-driven* organization within the school that serves as a
venue for students to create and implement projects and activities they believe are of timely social importance, and that will more deeply engage the
student body in the school's development and success. At any given time,
students are in the Center talking and eating lunch together, making buttons
and T-shirts (for fundraising), planning community-based events, organizing
workshops and after-school groups, and thinking of ways to encourage more
students to join them.

Indeed, at Parkway NW, students are involved in almost all aspects of the
school culture, including creating the school's codes of student conduct,
which, after significant debate, now include guidelines such as: respect everyone's opinion (nobody is "wrong"); learn how to take constructive criticism; stop jumping to conclusions; no laughing at or teasing others; and
speak wisely.

The school also highly values the process of self-reflection, underscoring
that being a leader and building social responsibility come through "exploring their own values and beliefs," and "taking greater responsibility for others." Students experiment with diverse methods of communicating and inter-
personal problem-solving, including traveling together on Outward Bound

trips, collaboratively organizing teach-ins and community fundraising events, and visiting other schools to teach them about service learning and to help them design their own peer-mediation programs.

In many ways the school still resembles a typical college preparatory program, with standards-based classes in math, science, social studies, and English. But Parkway has also experimented with interdisciplinary learning, such as the school's SHARE curriculum, designed by teachers in *S*panish, *H*istory, *A*rt, *R*esearch, and *E*nglish. Through SHARE, these teachers have worked together to thread common questions and themes through all of their classes, such as "What happens when students are aware of other cultures?"

Some of SHARE's activities have included a day-long community service project on Martin Luther King Day where students organized a teach-in and series of workshops for other students and community guests on topics such as cultural awareness, world hunger, peaceful protests, and global intercon-nectedness.

Significantly, like many of the extracurricular offerings at Parkway NW, this event is *student-initiated* and directed. For example, one student who took part in a seminar on gender roles began to notice how few males were involved with dance at the school. He went on to form a school wide black male dance group called *Aftershock* that now performs throughout the city. The group seeks to challenge stereotypes about urban black males by creat-ing improvisational and audience-interaction performances that show a range of emotions, expression, and movement.

Indeed, issues such as the impact of gender and sex roles are not only acknowledged in the school curriculum, they are actively addressed and highlighted. In 2009, for example, Parkway NW worked with the Wharton School at the University of Pennsylvania to organize a half-day seminar that included speakers on homosexuality, HIV/AIDS, and body-image disorders, as well as student performances in music, dance, poetry, and dramatic read-ing.

The school also houses All Acceptance Alliance, a student-run organiza-tion focused on gender and sexuality issues. Additionally, in 2009 more than ninety Parkway NW students participated in the thirteenth annual Day of Silence designed to show collective support for GLBTQ communities, and to openly reject the violence and oppression that members of these communities face.

The school is similarly explicit about promoting a multicultural curricu-lum, which encourages students to openly address, rather than silence, un-comfortable conversations about race and racism. Teachers don't just ask students to define *racism;*, they ask students to think critically about the forces that may have led to the *growth* and *institutionalization* of racism.

Given that the student body is nearly 100 percent African American, teachers recognize the need to help students feel comfortable making connections between racism in history and in students' lives.

Although Parkway NW centers many of its activities around the surrounding neighborhood, the school also organizes many special trips, such as regular visits to the United Nations, the Holocaust Museum, and overseas exchange programs. It's important to note, however, that although the school embraces a peace and social justice theme, its emphasis, as one former teacher underscores, "is on promoting alternatives to violence rather than opposition to government policies." She continues, "We have plenty of students here who have family involved in the [Iraq] war. So we don't take an official stand."

Indeed, many activities championed by the school offer opportunities for students and their families to support military personnel and veterans. In 2008, for example, the school sponsored a "Peaceful Knitting Circle," where students and family members knitted limb covers for people who had lost a limb in the war. This event was part of a school wide program called "Project Word," which included storytelling, dancing, poetry, and other activities that helped students better understand the experiences of people involved in active conflict in different countries and cultures. The Parkway Peace Choir sang songs from the civil rights era, while others attended sessions on social justice topics as diverse as the Holocaust and foster parenting.

And like the other schools profiled in this book, Parkway NW puts a strong emphasis on student critical inquiry, *even when that inquiry might lead to public criticisms of the school itself*. Through the Student Community Development Center, for example, students organized a Student Speak Out on the subject of "Oppression in Education at Parkway." This was a very rare opportunity for students to critique the practices of their own school, as well as how students, teachers, and administrators relate to one another. At the heart of the event was an opportunity to consider how the school community could address concerns that often get marginalized or silenced in the quest for order and efficiency. The event focused on *active listening* among students and staff, *collaborative problem-solving*, and *student-initiated innovations*.

Finally, it is important to note that the new focus on peace and social justice has not deterred the school from its college-preparatory beginnings. In the last five years, test scores at Parkway NW have risen, suspensions have decreased, attendance has increased, and the graduation rate is now close to 100 percent, with almost all students going to college. As Principal McGee writes about the school's rich and unusual transformation:

A few years ago . . . who would have foreseen students playing a major role in
safety through student led mediation and peer trainings in community development and service learning? *Who would have identified the above as methods of
achieving academic excellence, career exploration, college preparation, and
civic responsibility?* [1]

Following are examples of how teachers and students are embracing risk
together at Parkway NW.

EXAMPLE 1

"AIN'T I A . . .": EXPLORING THE POLITICS OF IDENTITY

You can't teach underprivileged children about social justice as if it were
purely a matter of memorizing equal-rights laws or discussing hypothetical
ethics. While African American history is required for ninth-graders in the
Philadelphia School District, teachers are free to approach it from many
different angles, and no two classes look alike. Even when the topics are the
same (e.g., the Underground Railroad, or the legacy of Dr. Martin Luther
King), the sources, assignments, pedagogical approaches, and critical questions range considerably.

When you have school where 99 percent of the students are African
American and you are a white teacher, it is easy to appear condescending or
to try to keep uncomfortable topics like slavery and racism in the framework
of the distant past. This does not work well, according to Parkway NW
history teacher Autumn Burdo. On the first day I visit her classroom, students are exploring a new set of vocabulary words:

- Fictive kin—fake family relationships
- Slave codes—law, rules for slaves
- Miscegenation—interracial sexual relations/consensual rape
- Assimilation—when minority feels like they have to fit into majority
  group
- Acculturation—when one culture picks things up about another culture
  and adapts

The teacher asks questions such as "How many of you have fictive kin?"
prompting a near 100 percent response as students wave their hands in the
air, waiting to tell their own stories. After discussing "dictionary definitions"
and the subtle differences between words like *assimilation* and *acculturation*,
Burdo gets to the heart of her lesson:

What does it *feel* like?

Burdo feels strongly that history has to be more than simply an exercise in memorizing facts and dates. Regardless whether you are part of the culture or historical events being studied, everyone has opinions, questions, and (often conflicting) feelings about it. Thus, the night's homework assignment:

> Assignment: For each vocabulary word, answer the question: What do these words "feel like" or "look like"?

Students are encouraged to engage in and draw on creative writing, memoirs, interviews, photographs, drawings, music . . . any way they can think of to represent the word so that it engages the heart as well as the brain. During the rest of class, students are asked to consider questions, such as: "What is hypocrisy?" "What are the consequences of hypocrisy?" "What is a moral dilemma?" After they have thought about the questions for a while, they work in small groups to compare their responses.

Throughout the semester, Burdo seeks ways to make African American history more meaningful and authentic to her students. For example, after reading *Ain't I a Woman?* Sojourner Truth's historic address at the Akron Women's Convention in 1851, students analyze and reflect on Truth's argument about race, gender, and equality. Burdo wanted her students to investigate the narrative form of Truth's address, comparing it to other kinds of narratives that people use in struggle and protest, and thinking about why this particular form was so effective and memorable.

She then wanted students to think beyond the historic situation of black women in the 1800s and critically explore how other kinds of identities have been marginalized, and how societies create and recreate the categories of "us" and "them," based on social and cultural capital. Students were thus given the following assignment:

> Think of a personal identity you struggle with the most. Write your own "Ain't I a . . ." speech explaining your struggles, the issues you face because of this identity, and how you think it can be overcome.

The range, creativity, and intensity of students' responses to this assignment showed that they were moved by Truth's speech and could relate to the larger themes of oppression and marginalization in their own lives. Student speeches included topics such as family ties, rites of passage, and mental health. For example:

Ain't I *the child of my parents?*

Ain't I the child of my parents? Mother and father. I don't feel like I have a father because I never really met my father before the age of 14. . . . He was a nice guy but not a good person. Two years past and we stopped talking. . . . Now my mother, I don't live with her anymore and haven't since the age of 13. Yeah, she loves me and I love her, but 8 years ago, only because she wanted me to get a better education [I moved out]. . . . I'm starting to feel unwanted in this life since the people who want me here are trying to kick me out of their hearts. Ain't I a child of my parents?

Ain't I a *teenager!*

When I wake up every morning at 8:30 am to get ready for school. Ain't I a Teenager! Yes sometimes I walk around with my nose in the air but Ain't I a teenager! I am always criticized for yelling at one person for something that wasn't even serious. Ain't I a teenager? I am an average 16 year old girl trying to juggle social life, home and school. Ain't I a teenager? Why would anyone penalize me for the very few times I act immature, because ain't I a teenager? Sometimes I sit tall and talk to my parents and teachers as if I was their age. Ain't I a teenager? Through all the good and bad, all the happy and sad, I hardly acknowledge this fact, but ain't I a teenager?

Ain't I a *human?*

I get up every morning and it's the same routine. Wash-up, put on my clothes, do my hair and eat, just like everybody else.

    Ain't I human?

    Just because I get more emotional more than others does that make me crazy?

    So I'm not suppose to show emotions?

    Shouldn't I be able to cry whenever I want, laugh whenever I want?

    I'm just being human.

    Is that so wrong?

EXAMPLE 2

NOT ALL SINGING AND DANCING: EXPANDING KNOWLEDGE ABOUT DIVERSITY, CULTURE, AND GLOBALISM

Parkway NW is clear about its commitment to globalism. Rather than teach about global history and current events as the United States versus everyone else, Parkway NW gets students to think about the complexity of cultural identity and of cultural change. One example takes place every year in Geoffrey Winikur's tenth-grade English class. It begins with a film called *Moolaadé*. Viewing the film has become something of a "classic" experience at Parkway NW; students from previous years still come back to tell him what an effect the film had on them, and to talk with students seeing the film for the first time.

Winikur begins by telling students they are free to get up and (quietly) leave the room any time they are too uncomfortable. In this age of shoot-up action vampire zombie films, it's hard for students to imagine what topic could be so difficult to watch. *Moolaadé* ("magical protection") is a 2004 film that graphically addresses the subject of female genital cutting, a common practice in many African countries. Girls as young as twelve are required to be purified by undergoing this operation without anesthesia. Many die in the process.

The circumcision is sometimes performed by the girl's mother and/or female relatives, while the father stands outside the door as a symbolic gesture to protect the process. The girls scream in pain and often try to commit suicide. The process is considered a prerequisite for marriage. Those who live suffer from lifelong pain, especially when they have sexual intercourse or urinate. The process also decreases women's fertility and ability to carry a child to term. The primary purpose of the ritual—which cuts across ethnicities and religions—is to keep women from wanting to cheat on their husbands.

Moolaadé, while fictional, is based on real life, and was set and filmed in a remote village in West Africa. The plot involves a wife and mother, Colle, who has been cut and does not want her daughter to experience the same pain and grief. Colle ends up protecting her own daughter, as well as several other young girls in the village, by shielding the girls in her house and using witchcraft—including draping the colorful rope of Moolaadé across the gate—to curse anyone who tries to take the girls out of the house. One mother takes her daughter out of the house, and the daughter dies in the operation, causing other mothers to question the tradition.

The film also follows the struggle of Colle's own daughter, who is engaged to be married but doesn't want to be cut. Colle's husband, believing he has lost control of his wife, beats her mercilessly. The men in the village do everything they can to stop change, including burning all the radios so women cannot learn things or get ideas about equality from the outside world. It would be easy to use the film to reinforce the notion that primitive cultures have no respect for human rights or, specifically, women's rights. The film, however, presents a much more complex story. As one critic wrote:

Unlike many recent Hollywood made films about Africa, *Moolaadé* is a story about Africa made by Africans from a distinctly local perspective. Yet, it speaks to universal themes of power, oppression, and emancipation. In depicting one woman's struggle to protect others from an oppressive and inhibiting tradition, Sembene brings great sensitivity and nuance to topic that is often discussed from simplistic, patronizing, and polarizing standpoints. He deftly explores not only the conflict between local traditional values and the influence of modern ideas, but also the gender and generational tensions within a community largely isolated from the outside world.[2]

Winikur uses the film to raise much broader discussions than simply whether it is "right" or "wrong" to mutilate females for the purposes of purity and marriageability. Though most students agree that genital mutilation is, in fact, wrong, Winikur asks them to think about larger issues of law versus tradition, cultural preservation and change, how conflict is intertwined with power, and how change comes from both within and without the confines of a single culture. This includes addressing the impact of technology on expanding sources of information and dialogue to communities previously living in near-isolation.

Winikur also asks students to think about strategies for struggle, human rights activism, survival and protection of others, negotiating tactics, and solving difficult moral dilemmas. At heart, the lesson is about *point of view* and the idea that what seems obviously wrong to one group of people may appear entirely rational and justified to another.

Winikur shows the film over a period of days, so that he has time to stop it at various junctures and ask for students' reactions or questions about particular scenes or events. It is an interactive process, where students practice the skills of critical analysis and empathy simultaneously. In one assignment, for example, students write letters from the point of view of different characters in the film, defending their position on female mutilation regardless of the student's own position.

Student essays bring forth some of the conflicts that the film raises:

I think it focuses on issues that people don't generally talk about. It was informational but a little disturbing. This movie focuses on how women don't always have freedom of speech . . . It will also give [viewers] an account of how African culture is not all about music and dance.

This way of being "purified" goes against all rights for women. It's like saying that women don't have power over their bodies. Everybody should be able to control his or her body. . . . This type of movie showed me that if you stand up for what you believe and keep fighting it is sure to happen eventually.

From this movie I learned that standing up and speaking out for what you believe is wrong can have great results in the end. . . . I also learned that even if you don't succeed then keep trying until you get what you want. I am tired of people who don't succeed and then want to blame it on someone else. Just shut up, suck it up, and move on with life.

Colle was resistant to the powerful pounds of his whip because of her loyalty to those girls. She believed that what she believed in was the truth, and she was determined to prove her point. By any means necessary. Colle was a warrior and was given that title at the end of the movie by her actions. *Moolaadé* is a story of dignity, respect, and loyalty. That was the brilliance of this text.

To be honest, I thought the movie was going to be a boring documentary, but I was wrong. . . . Many things can be learned from watching *Moolaadé*. Law, power, and traditions are only a few of them. This is a very powerful movie and it shows that anything you set your mind to can be done if you stand up for what you believe in. By doing that, change may come your way.

EXAMPLE 3

EXPLORING *AND ADDRESSING* WORLD CHALLENGES

Many other classes at Parkway NW address globalism in a similar way, with the intent of going beyond issues of right and wrong, winning and losing, power, privilege, domination, and weakness. One class, for example, focuses on "world challenges." Students receive two questions to frame their work over the semester: (1) What are the world challenges in 2011? And (2) How can we discover these challenges?

A detailed assignment follows:

- Your first task is to research a country and learn about that country. As you collect information about the country, you should use the following questions to guide your research:
- What are some interesting facts about the country? (Collect information about the country—history, current population, climate, natural resources, economy, political situation, etc.)
- What do most people do for a living? What kinds of jobs exist in the country? Are most people employed? Is it a poor country? A well-to-do country?
- What are the challenges that people face in this country? Describe them and explain them in some detail.

- What is the MOST IMPORTANT challenge facing this country? Why is it so important? Describe the country and challenges in your own words. Paint a picture so that others can understand the country and its challenges.

After you have collected this information and written in your own words, you will write a report about that country that answers the questions above, and then share this information with others who have researched other countries in the same area of the world. Together you will decide on THREE MOST COMMON CHALLENGES FACING THESE COUNTRIES. You will have a chance to share information about your countries in your area of the world and the three challenges you identify together.

- Your second task will be to examine one of the challenges facing the world today and learn about it in great detail. You will also examine ways to help find solutions to the challenges facing the world. You should use the following questions to help guide your research about this challenge:
- What is the challenge? Describe and explain the challenge in your own words.
- How common is the challenge? Where is it found? (Is it global? Primarily found in some areas? Some countries?)
- How serious is the challenge? Is it a long-term challenge? A life-threatening challenge?
- Who is working to solve the challenge? What individuals? What groups? How are they trying to solve the challenge?
- What obstacles are there in solving this challenge?
- What are your own suggestions for solving this challenge? How would you go about trying to solve this problem?

You will create a poster that lists and explains the challenge, describes where it is located, explains who is working on this challenge and what is being done to solve it, and suggests one or more solutions to the challenge. The posters will be shared in class and also hung in the hallways so that everyone in the school can become familiar with the challenges facing the United States and the world today.

Students are assigned to focus on countries across the globe, in Africa, Asia, Middle East, Latin and South America, and Europe.

More traditional schools would likely tell students what world challenges are most important (rather than letting them research and decide for themselves), and then assign the challenges to students regardless of their interests. Moreover, the comparison would traditionally be between the country in question and the United States, rather than looking at the way certain challenges are faced across many different countries, and, more importantly, are deeply affected by global interaction and decisions made by countries with greater power, resources, or other leverage.

Finally, it is worth noting that students work on this assignment in groups, learning about the impact of collaboration and compromise at the same time they are experiencing it. As they seek to come up with solutions to their challenges, they are encouraged to find more than one solution, suggesting that there are many different ways to address conflicts and many roles for different groups of people to play in this process.

EXAMPLE 4

STUDENTS TEACHING STUDENTS

Indeed, the role of student collaboration at Parkway NW (like all the schools described in this book) should not be minimized. Students not only work together in groups and "share out," but also even help teach the class and design quizzes that their fellow students will take and be graded on. An example of this is found in Rachel King-Davis's world religions class. Working in groups, students choose to study one religion from the following list:

- Hinduism
- Buddhism
- Taoism
- Daoism
- Judaism
- Christianity
- Islam
- Confucianism

Each group then researches the following questions:

Find out the origins of this group.
What did they believe?
Who are their gods/deity?
What are their most important (sacred) texts?
What impact does this religion have on people?

An important direction for students as they approach this assignment is to "put the answers in your own words, don't just quote from religious leaders and texts." King-Davis wants students to think about deeper meaning and to deconstruct the language of speeches and ideologies that are often written to persuade people to act in a certain way or embrace a certain value.

After students complete this first leg of the assignment, they make a group PowerPoint presentation for the rest of the class, teaching about the religion they studied. King-Davis says one of the primary reasons she takes this approach is because students are always complaining that "history is boring." She believes that having students teach each other is a way to get them to be more engaged.

On the day I visited, the student presentations were over, but students were assigned to reflect on what they'd done: the process of working in a group, preparing presentations, teaching the class, and listening to other students teach. Interestingly, many students said that they felt fully prepared to present but "clammed up" when the time came to stand in front of their peers. The teacher used this as an opportunity to get student input on ways to present besides PowerPoint. One group of students suggested that they present in a Jeopardy-style quiz format, which they thought would be more interactive and more "exciting." The teacher agreed to let them try it next time.

Students also asked whether the quizzes that they were asked to create and distribute to their classmates (based on their presentations) would truly count toward their grade. It seemed inconceivable to most students that they would have this kind of power. The teacher assured them that the quizzes would count. "You taught the lesson," she said. "So, yes, it's a real quiz!"

EXAMPLE 5

COMING HOME AGAIN: (RE)INVESTING IN THE COMMUNITY

In the 2010–2011 school year, one of the cross-disciplinary thematic questions that all students at Parkway NW were to address was "What is Philadelphia?" In the mandatory Social Leadership class for ninth- and tenth-graders, teacher King-Davis brought in students from the University of Pennsylvania's Wharton School of Business to work with Parkway NW students weekly as they produced a series of virtual museum exhibits around the question: "What makes Mt. Airy so special?" (Mt. Airy is the section of the city where the Parkway NW school is located.)

After forming students into groups of five and matching each group with a Wharton student, King-Davis assigned each group to examine a different slice of what defines Mt. Airy. Some groups, for example, focused on history, others on the community's economy, others on the different cultures represented in the community, and still others on the school's founding and its relationship to the community itself. Students then began brainstorming a list of questions they wanted to learn more about.

Next, King-Davis showed the class a short documentary about Mt. Airy as an example of what they might do themselves. Yet she was careful to elicit their ideas and input, asking students critical questions such as: *Does this film have a particular point of view? Do you think the filmmakers made conscious decisions as to what parts of the community to film, and what times of day to film at that location? What voices and experiences were NOT represented in this film? What questions does it leave you wanting to know more about?* After discussing these questions as a class, students went back to their small groups and began to formalize plans for their video projects.

The group focusing on culture and diversity, for example, formulated the following list of questions to ask community members as they taped them:

- What were people wearing way "back in the day"?
- Do you think Mt. Airy is violent?
- Do you think people believe Mt. Airy is a bad place?
- Does Mt. Airy have a lot to do with the history of Philadelphia?
- If you had one word to describe Mt. Airy, what would it be?
- What are the greatest challenges of Mt. Airy?
- Do you think Mt. Airy is overcrowded?
- Do you think Mt. Airy is respectful of diverse cultures and traditions?
- In your opinion, (how) did Mt. Airy improve over the years?

Similarly, the group of students who were looking at the relationship between the history of their school and the larger community wanted to know:

- Why did they change Amy Northwest to Parkway Northwest?
- Why did the location switch?
- What was the main reason for creating Parkway NW?
- Why did the creator of Parkway NW add "peace and social justice"?
- How long did it take to construct this school?
- Why are so many schools on this campus?
- Why did some schools decide *not* to be on this campus?
- Why did they decide to take away the school for the Deaf and Special Education?
- Who built the dam/river near the gym?

- What were the rules and codes of conduct of Parkway NW back in the 1990s?
- What's the oldest building on campus?
- Is this campus a place where war took place long ago?

Having made a list of questions, students began brainstorming how they were going to approach making their video. The conversation at each table was flooded with ideas. As part of the assignment, students were to assign specific roles in the group, much like real filmmakers and historians. In other words, one person would be chiefly responsible for asking questions, another for the filming and/or editing, another for research and source checking, another for raising funds to make the video, and another for promoting it to the rest of the school and the community at large.

Not only were the resulting videos impressively researched and critically framed and narrated, but student responses to the process were extremely positive. One student said, for example: "All the buildings that I pass every-day actually have meaning now. I learned how many important things have happened here in Philadelphia in my community." Another student echoed this sentiment: "This project is benefiting me because I know more about the history of our school's neighborhood. I live in this community and by doing this type of work, I see the good and the bad in the community."

Students also felt that working with Wharton students "makes our work seem more official," and that the people they interviewed for their films (say, directors of historic sites) "took us more seriously because the Wharton students were our partners." Parkway NW students saw this as a two-way process, however. They hoped that the Wharton students would benefit from the opportunity to "get to know how us younger people look at things," and that "it will help broaden their horizons." One student hoped that: "When they go back to Wharton, they will look at things differently from the way they used to. Now maybe they can apply their new knowledge to their business work in the future." This is a meaningful example of how what happens in the classroom does not need to stay in the classroom; learning is essentially as multifaceted, multidirectional process that can genuinely include the community.

QUESTIONS TO CONSIDER:

- Do you think that having a school organized around the themes of "peace" and "social justice" is comparable to having a school organized around a more traditional academic subject, such as science, a "skill" like architecture, or a "talent" such as the performing arts? What makes certain topics and kinds of knowledge more likely to be labeled "political," "ideological," or "biased"?

- How are the themes of "peace," "social justice," "globalism," "activism," and "community" addressed in your curriculum? In what ways are they taught as (a) *vocabulary* words to be learned; (b) *concepts* to be debated and explored; and/or (c) *values* to be contested or embraced?
- Does the curriculum at your school attempt to make connections between these various concepts? How? Do you have examples of bridging lessons about a historic event, or a transformative moment in a particular culture's history, with broader questions about social leadership, interaction, justice, culture, communication, and social change?
- In what ways does your school try to make connections between disciplinary content and students' own experiences? For example, what opportunities exist in your school for students to safely explore and express their own experiences with violence, oppression, marginalization, inequity, silencing, and/or victimization?
- Likewise, what opportunities exist in your school for students to openly *challenge* cultural stereotypes, traditions, political systems, and public policies that they do not agree with or find personally demeaning?
- Is teaching students about social leadership, and giving them opportunities to engage in social leadership, something that your school values as part of a "good education"? Should social leadership become an official part of a school's accountability, and if so, how would we assess it?
- Finally, how is the concept of "leadership" more generally a part of your school's mission and explicit or implicit curriculum? What is the range of definitions of "leadership" among staff and students at your school? Specifically, what qualities are associated with leadership (strength, power, charisma, self-discipline, good judgment, ethical fitness, strong communication skills, active listening skills, mediation skills, etc.)?

NOTES

1. From *Parkway NW Winter 2009 Newsletter* (emphasis mine).
2. Bonny Ibhawoh, McMaster University, Canada, May 18, 2010.

Chapter Five

Unlocking the Schoolyard Gate: Geography, Community, and Risk

The Wissahickon Charter School

The heart of our curriculum is inquiry into the outside world by students and teachers, and active engagement to leave the world better than we found it. . . . Our interest is not just to study what is. We also ask students to imagine what should be and what could be while actively making it so.
—Wissahickon Charter School website

This chapter explores the Wissahickon Charter School, a nine-year-old K–8 charter school that integrates environmental education, activism, and eco-literacy across the curriculum. Using inquiry-based, hands-on, collaborative teaching and learning as the school norm, the school seeks to "provide a community of learning with an environmental focus that stimulates the child's intellectual, social and character development."

The school was founded by a diverse group of community activists and educators, who wanted to give city children unique opportunities to explore the stories and histories within their own urban communities, while at the same time learning to navigate a wide variety of natural and rural settings. The school promotes a "discovery-based approach" to all learning, cultivating and underscoring values such as curiosity, critical inquiry, respect for evidence, flexibility, and sensitivity to living things.

The Wissahickon Charter School embraces risk by redefining the boundaries of the classroom and textbook learning to include student-centered action research and sustained interaction with resources in the surrounding community. This includes, for example, daily engagement in the school's working garden, a healthy lunch program, and an adjoining natural park.

103

Moreover, the school is committed to a curriculum that gives children access to environments that are typically less accessible to inner-city students (woods, lakes, and mountains). The school seeks to create an ethical context for learning that stresses environmental awareness, community service, global communication, and human connections in sustaining life on Earth.

THE WISSAHICKON CHARTER SCHOOL AT A GLANCE

- Eco-centered whole-school focus on environmental justice, peace, and globalism.
- Experiential learning, including many trips to diverse urban and rural locations (overnight camping trips, working on farms, hiking trips, Outward Bound expeditions).
- School–community connections (e.g., building playgrounds, improving use of/accessibility to natural space in urban environment, in-service program, building sustainable cities).
- "Purposeful Investigation": an interdisciplinary, project-based approach to learning that builds on essential questions and problem-solving over the course of a semester.
- School-community garden, composting and recycling program; daily use of neighboring nature center.
- Recognition of diverse learning styles and close attention to the social interaction and community-building.
- Strong parental involvement in all aspects of school.
- Demographics: 95 percent African American, 4 percent white, 1 percent Hispanic; 80 percent students eligible for free or reduced-price lunch programs.

LIVING THE CURRICULUM

By 10:30 a.m. on a rainy Friday morning, the entire student body is seated in the school cafeteria, waiting for Philadelphia's mayor, Michael Nutter. The occasion: The Wissahickon Charter School's first Sustainable Cities Summit. Seventh- and eighth-grade students, dressed in their best, exchange excited whispers, curious about the fifteen other invited guests who have yet to introduce themselves. The school's co-CEO Kristi Littell takes the stage and tells the students that the people they will meet and talk with today represent the "meaning and applicability" of what they have been doing all year in school. "These folks are living out your curriculum." What does she mean?

For months, students have been working in groups to design and build their own environmentally friendly, sustainable cities. Indeed, since last September, seventh- and eighth-graders have been studying all aspects of cities, including issues of clean water and alternative energy, housing, education, health and safety, zoning, taxation and city revenue, and business development. They have closely compared American cities with those in the Middle East and East Asia, studied the path water takes from their school to the Atlantic Ocean, and visited city structures and neighborhoods in Philadelphia.

More recently, students used the computer game *Sim City* to simulate their own city visions and plans. Now, with their 2D blueprints and plans in hand, they are ready to move toward building their cities with reused materials on three-foot-by-three-foot lots. With the help of their teachers, the students could easily have gone forward with their city-building without much additional preparation, yet today represents an important step in the learning process. Students are meeting with area professionals whose lives are devoted to making cities more sustainable. Invited guests include representatives from governmental and nonprofit entities such as the Philadelphia Industrial Development Corporation, Awbury Arboretum, Recycle Bank, the Energy Coordinating Agency, and SEPTA (Philadelphia's primary public transportation system).

Also present are entrepreneurs who founded and directed organizations such as Philly Rooted, which reclaims vacant city land for agricultural use, employing city youth in the process; Mt. Airy USA, which counsels first-time homebuyers; Clean Markets, a market and business-development firm; GreenMicrofinance.org, an environmental education organization with an interest in socially responsible investing, savvy consuming, and philanthropy; and the Trolley Car Diner, a nearby restaurant that uses green energy and locally grown food, and has contributed over $100,000 to community groups.

Rounding out the guest list is a variety of urban architects, gardeners and landscapers, and, of course, Mayor Nutter himself. Inviting the mayor to open the day's events was more than a publicity ploy. Mayor Nutter helped the Wissahickon Charter School get its operating license back when he was still on the city council, and he is implementing a plan to make Philadelphia the greenest U.S. city by 2015.

When the mayor arrives, he looks proudly on the student body and proclaims: "If you're looking at these issues in seventh and eighth grade, you're going to be able to handle the mess we are making [in the environment]. I believe that someone in this room will be the inventor of sustainable energy in years to come."

After the introductions, the guests disperse to classrooms to meet with small groups of students who will present their city plans, get critical feedback, answer questions, and, perhaps most importantly, ask questions of their own. While students are eager to learn more about building cities from the perspective of those who do it every day, they are also excited to think that some of their ideas might actually be "good enough" to be taken back to the guests' organizations and presented as viable new directions, projects, solutions, and/or alternatives.

The students' city plans differ considerably. Though all the groups were challenged to think about the place of residential housing, industry, small businesses, and natural resources, their decisions were framed by larger questions about what *kind* of city they hoped to build. For example, one group wants to build mostly communal housing, which would use fewer resources per person. Others discuss storage systems for saving water, how food would be brought into the city (e.g., homegrown vs. imported), and how the city would make public spaces most accessible and inviting to a broad range of residents of different ages, interests, and physical abilities.

Students' questions touch on issues such as overpopulation, waste production, safety, education and equity. One group of students says, for example, that they are very concerned about poor people in their city. They ask a thoughtful question: "Would it be more cost-effective to give poor people free education, health care, and housing as they needed it, than to risk increased crime and skyrocketing costs of social services down the road?"

Students are likewise concerned about how to keep their cities from being overpopulated, how close homes and businesses should be to one another, and what kinds of public transportation should be available. The details range from preventing factory windmills from blowing pollution into residential areas, to zoning that would forbid someone to build a factory directly next to a house or school.

One issue that comes up in a number of groups is whether to have separate areas of the city designated for business and for housing. In each case, guests ask students to think about what would happen to the business area after the stores close for the day. Would it be largely deserted? Would this increase crime and a sense that the downtown was not safe? Would this, in turn, discourage new businesses from opening? They use concrete examples, from Philadelphia and Baltimore, to tell the stories of how other cities learned from similar mistakes and eventually reorganized to become more socially integrated.

The day is designed so that students have the opportunity both to present and to listen to their classmates' presentations. They also have numerous opportunities to work with guests so that they can benefit from a broad range of expertise and insight. At the end of the event, students and guests share food and talk informally. Students can take great pride in the planning they accomplish, while recognizing that a sustainable city needs input from a broad range of engaged experts and community members working cooperatively, and with an open mind.

As they do with other thematic projects at the Wissahickon Charter School, students needed to draw upon and make connections among their content knowledge of math, economics, science, technology, public policy, history, reading, writing, and design, while keeping in mind larger questions about social and environmental justice, cultural diversity, and globalism. This let them to go beyond rote memorization into a new kind of learning in which they gained valuable skills in problem-solving, working collaboratively, imagining and creating in a number of different mediums, critical reflection and thoughtful revision, and sustained commitment and empathy.

Thinking about *quality of life* is, in fact, an integral part of the school curriculum at the Wissahickon Charter School. Both the formal and informal curriculum stress showing respect for others and building personal relationships. The idea is that the school is much more than a "factory" of learning; it is a genuine community that must be nurtured and sustained. Students are intricately involved in important decisions regarding how to make the school a more inviting and engaging community for everybody involved. They've even been known to rearrange the classroom furniture.

"A SOFT LANDING"

When you walk into the Wissahickon Charter School, one of the first things you notice is that the extra-wide hallways are filled with comfy couches, populated by students of many different ages sitting alone or in pairs, studying quietly or discussing an upcoming project or trip. Throughout the day, students walk through the hallways, usually with their classmates and friends, but not in straight lines. Nor are they silent. They are talking and laughing, sharing stories, ribbing each other, waving hello to their younger siblings.

Yet their conduct is far from unruly or "wild." The school's mission statement says that "the greatest cognitive growth occurs through social interaction." Drawing on an educational resource called the "Responsive Classroom", the school teaches students important social skills such as cooperation, assertion, responsibility, empathy, and self-control. The school practices a pedagogy called "Guided Discovery" that not only "encourages inquiry" but also emphasizes responsibility and "care of the school environment."

Inside the classrooms, teachers call students "my friends," and they circle the room as they talk and join students' small-group discussions. All the classrooms are designed to accommodate collaborative learning; there are many tables but no rows of desks. In one middle-school science class, two of the students are sitting cross-legged on what is essentially a counter, with their laptops in their laps. In the younger grades, kids are spontaneously stretching. A third-grade girl is standing up at her desk, wiggling and dancing with a big smile on her face. If the noise level gets too high, teachers will ring a bell, and students immediately quiet down and refocus their attention on the teacher.

One day a science teacher arrived a few minutes late from a meeting and observed that the class, though seated, was not focused on the day's assignment. "I don't mean this as a punishment," he began, "but why don't we all stand up, walk out into the hallway, and come back into the classroom." The students gracefully rose up and shuffled out into the hallway. When they returned, they sat more quietly at their desks, looking at the teacher for the next direction.

At Wissahickon, every classroom begins the day with a morning meeting (also called "Circle of Power and Respect" in middle school). This ritual is what the Responsive Classroom model refers to as "a soft landing" to the school day. According to Littell, "Students are warmly greeted, they play a game or do an activity, there is a chance to share and ask each other questions, and there is a message from the teacher." The larger goal is to engage kids in the coming school day, help everyone to get to know each other better, and build a sense of community. The activities range from throwing a ball, acting out a scene from a play, or reflecting as a group on an academic question or personal problem.

In one class, for example, the teacher asked the students to think about what they do when they make a "mistake" (make excuses or lie, make retribution, give up trying, etc.) and to share their strategies with the larger group. Then they talked as a class about how to "recover" from mistakes rather than let them depress or defeat you. Students appeared interested in what their classmates had to say, and in strategies they had not previously thought about.

The "Talk It Out" method is staple of the school. Instead of teachers and administrators imposing a list of rules that focus primarily on punishment, the students volunteer to work together with teachers over recess to create what the school calls *social guidelines*. The school consciously works with students to discuss ways of solving problems and working together to make the school feel like a safe and inviting community for everyone.

When there are conflicts, students are asked to think about what they need. Is it an apology? Does something need to be changed or fixed? Was there a misunderstanding? According to Littell: "'Talk It Out' is explicitly taught as a program that gives students a framework for working through conflict. They learn to use *I* statements, to take turns speaking, to work toward a shared resolution."

Wissahickon, in fact, was built on the idea that "the social curriculum is as important as the academic curriculum." This means that the *process* of learning goes hand in hand with the content. Adults are expected to model a process of open-minded inquiry and respect for diversity. Likewise, adults approach one another and their students with a genuine interest in collaboration. The school even has two CEOs (a white woman and a black man) to model the importance of diversity and working together.

Students are encouraged to look critically and with a sense of ownership at all aspects of the school. They begin each year by talking about their hopes and dreams—what do they want for themselves and their class during the year? Sometimes the answers involve academic achievement ("I want to learn algebra") or another personal milestone ("I want to make new friends," "I want to learn to grow melons in the community garden," or "I want to learn to swim or climb a mountain").

They are not all "I" statements, however. Students are encouraged to talk about how they want to interact as a community and what goals they share in common. Then they communally plan how to help each other meet their individual and shared goals. Nothing is off-limits in this discussion. Even something as seemingly "tangential" as the way the classroom is arranged is significant. Students are encouraged to think critically about how something as simple as where they sit can change the direction of learning. Then they can help rearrange the classroom and displays "to encourage independence, promote caring and maximize learning."

Asked to define the concept of *embracing risk* in education, Littell responded:

> When people speak of risk in education, we're always stuck that the meaning of risk can vary so widely. To some, what we do seems "risky." We teach in a hands-on way. We want our students to be leaders in their own education. We believe the social curriculum is as important as the academic curriculum, and that creating a community of learners is what yields curious critical thinkers. We believe that every adult in our building is a teacher and models our ideals daily. To us, the risks of not approaching education in this way are much greater.

The school emphasizes interdisciplinary learning, knowledge growing from real experience and the interconnectedness of physical and human environments. One of its primary values for all students and staff is "a critical stance and active engagement in the world."

A WHOLE-SCHOOL FOCUS ON THE ENVIRONMENT AND COMMUNITIES

One of Wissahickon's main goals to teach students about the environment and sustainability. To do this, the school created an interdisciplinary curriculum that blends academic skills and content with broader social questions and themes about the ways that humans interact locally and globally. This includes critical inquiry into understanding oneself and one's own values, as well as gaining a deep understanding of how humans have interacted throughout history, and how students can help solve contemporary conflicts. These are the themes for each grade, and some of the topics and activities they include:

Kindergarten: Ourselves and Our Communities

- Learning about students' individual experiences and interests, including writing "Me Books" along with a personal "Picture Dictionary"
- Interviewing community members about their jobs
- Mapping the classroom—understanding that the way things are arranged affects how they are used
- Life cycles of living things/the interdependence of the human and natural environments

First Grade: Neighborhoods

- Focus on trash and where it goes
- "How we can be heroes in our own neighborhood?" (doing service learning projects related to neighborhood study)
- Learning about mapping: neighborhoods, weather graphing, etc.
- Writing persuasive letters to help enact change

Second Grade: Neighborhoods (wider view)

- Where does our food come from—both in students' own neighborhoods and around the globe?
- Understanding nutrition and using this to improve how the school eats
- Learning about clothing production, from farm to factory
- Working in the school's own garden, and thinking about ways to use the garden not just for the school but for the community

Third Grade: City

- Economics, civics and the government, and geography of Philadelphia

- "How can we make the classroom more like the city of Philadelphia?"
- Immigration to Philadelphia/oral histories
- Transportation systems

Fourth Grade: State

- Prehistory of Pennsylvanians/Native Americans; colonial history
- Modern Pennsylvania, including railroads, climate change, coal as a resource, cultural conflict
- Biographies (e.g., Ben Franklin/Coal Miner's Bride), personal narratives, and realistic fiction
- Types of energy: renewable and nonrenewable

Fifth Grade: Country

- "We are the People"—study of the federal government, with a focus on the situation of minorities
- Colonization, the American Revolution and slavery
- U.S. and world geography and mapping skills
- U.S. ecosystems
- Connecting with pen pals in other states

Sixth Grade: Ancient Civilizations

- Precivilization, Ancient Egypt, and Greece
- Astronomy/astrology
- Museum trips
- Mythology of Ancient Greece
- Vocabulary: Greek root words

Seventh and Eighth Grade (Mixed): Year 1, Global Studies

- Latin America—history (colonialism), geography, natural resources
- East and Southeast Asia—history, geography, dynasties through urbanization
- The Middle East, with a focus on Israeli–Palestinian conflict
- Current events
- United Nations—research projects on International Human Rights
- Sustainable Cities Summit

Seventh and Eighth Grade (Mixed): Year 2, Twentieth-Century U.S. History

- Industrialization
- Family history research, interpreting primary source documents
- Race and justice—education, key Supreme Court cases, bias in race science, genetics and racial categories, memoirs and mentor texts
- Playgrounds—design and building
- Electoral system

PURPOSEFUL INVESTIGATION

> We have found that a great investigation needs something to make it go—something purposeful for students to work on and focus their inquiry.
> —Wissahickon School Curriculum Overview

As early as first grade, Wissahickon Charter School students are putting theory into action. As they study the surrounding neighborhood and, in particular, the process of disposing of trash there, they are given a concrete challenge: "Reduce the amount of waste that the school produces." This challenge has led students to start a whole system of composting in the school lunchrooms. The majority of students have shared what they are doing with their families, who are making similar changes at home.

Second- and third-graders are soon introduced to the school's garden, which they visit regularly. Their work in the garden is neither an extended recess nor a chore; it is an integral part of the school's academic curriculum. Students participate in a guided discussion about what they are seeing, as well as how they envision the garden growing and its possible uses. In garden journals, they will draw and write their ideas over the weeks to come; they will routinely use these journals for group sharing and reflection on the day's learning.

While working in the garden, students spend many weeks learning about key issues such as seasonality, soil types and structure, recycling, composting, and planting seeds and bulbs. For example, students observe three types of soil, recording differences in their appearance, color, smell, and texture in their journals. They then consider and record what happens to each type of soil when water is added to it. In a lesson on building soil structure, students learn about soil layers, topsoil, subsoils, fragmented rock, and bedrock before taking part in a hands-on activity where they are given ingredients to make their own model of soil structure. They use chocolate chips, crumbled Oreos, chocolate and butterscotch pudding, and graham cracker crumbs to construct the different layers, eventually adding gummy worms to the top.

Lessons are supplemented by reading relevant fiction and nonfiction texts, including *Planting a Garden, Compost!, The Magic School Bus Meets the Rot Squad*, and *Dirt, One Scoop of Soil*. After reading *Diary of a Worm*, for example, students make their own worm diary, writing from a worm's perspective. Not only must they think scientifically about how a worm survives and navigates its environment; they also get to practice creative writing, and in particular, using empathy and humor. This is a great example of weaving science and literacy together.

By fourth grade, students are studying every aspect of "water" in our lives, and go on monthly hikes to Wissahickon Creek. In past years, fourth-grade students have also worked together to participate in a service-learning project connected to their study of Fern Hill Park (a fifty-acre park across the street from the school). Students work with the staff of the Fairmount Park Commission to write a survey and collect data on human uses of the park. The survey solicits ideas for making the park more accessible and inviting for humans, while at the same time considering the protection and restoration of its natural ecosystem. In addition to improving their research, writing, and literacy skills, this project engages them in statistical analysis and complex problem-solving across the disciplines.

In middle school, students take part in the Sustainable Cities Project (mentioned at the beginning of the chapter), community service, and *action research projects*. Following are two more detailed examples of the kind of multistage course units that are emblematic of the school's pedagogy. In both assignments, students begin their investigation with something they encounter and interact with every day. As they start to look at what was once "routine" with new eyes, they begin to formulate questions that they can carry across different classes. Teachers work closely together to help students make connections and ask larger questions that bridge disciplines.

EXAMPLE 1

THE FULL SCOOP

Throughout the school year, second-graders at Wissahickon work together to explore the essential question: *Where does food come from?* The crux of this multifaceted assignment is to compare ways that people acquire food—from their own gardens, small businesses, the supermarket, and food co-ops. This interdisciplinary project connects aspects of second-grade math, science, social studies, and language arts.

Age-appropriate, creative, and hands-on activities in this unit include having students make "flip-books," where they draw the food items their families buy in each section of the supermarket; create a survey to learn more about people's favorite foods; and collaboratively create a lunch plan with items from all of the food groups and vote on which items will be included.

The class also plans and makes a class meal, something that most second-graders enjoy eating: pizza. First they examine the food groups involved. The students then work in small groups to choose a recipe and create a shopping list and a budget. In the process, they learn about ingredients and measurements and how to read food labels. Students also examine the "chemical names" of different ingredients and consider why chemicals might be added to certain foods.

Students then travel to different sites in the community, including warehouses and loading docks, to understand more about how stores acquire food. They consider where different ingredients are produced and find those sites on a map. They critically examine the production and transportation of food, which they document in an original mapmaking activity. While learning about the differences between a city, state, and country, students measure the distances that foods travel, study the ways that food is transported, and learn about the connection to pollution.

Students then discuss both the positive and negative consequences of getting food from "far away." Students watch a *Sesame Street* video about a boy on a farm making cheese and compare it to a *Food Network* video of how cheese is made in a factory. They then create flow charts showing the steps involved. They also write a song or a poem about how wheat is made into bread, or a "diary" of a wheat grain.

Students read fiction and nonfiction children's books about how sap becomes syrup, how a sheep's wool is used to make a sweater, and different cultural traditions around food. The teacher reads aloud the classic children's story *Charlotte's Web*, after which students are asked to "write a persuasive piece from one character to another explaining whether Wilber [the pig in the story] should be turned into bacon."

The class takes a trip to a local supermarket and a food co-op (including a farm where they help harvest food and take it directly to the co-op). Students make diagrams comparing the size of the two institutions; how food is processed; how food gets there; the number and type of products available, and whether they are organic; the time of year that different foods are available; and how food stays fresh.

They also compare who sells the food, the conditions under which they work, and methods of compensation. When they are finished, they pick one comparison from the chart they've made and illustrate it in greater detail. Students also create and implement their own surveys around the question of "why families shop where they do."

The assignment does not stop there. Students learn about literal photographs and mental snapshots, and are then asked to "remember a special meal" with their family and to draw as many details as possible. They use descriptive writing to go with the snapshots, for example, using adjectives to describe tastes. After students write their "family food stories," they read them aloud to each other and consider together the ways that food is an integral part of different families and cultures.

This is followed by a more systemic study of food traditions and rituals in different families around the world. They look at images drawn from the book *Hungry Planet*, which are hung museum-style around the classroom. Students travel around the classroom recording their thoughts and observations in the form of "I notice . . . ," "I feel . . . ," "I wonder . . . ," which leads to a class discussion. What images did they see in more than one picture? What did they see that they had never seen before? Which pictures looked most like what their own family eats? Which looked most different?

Then, working in pairs, they take a closer look at a picture of a family from another culture and brainstorm why the family is eating so many xxx? As they consider food in different cultures, they also make connections to their own cultures, using food as a way of understanding that American culture is not homogeneous. They discuss questions such as: What do you notice about the American family compared to most of the others? Why do you think they have so much food? Do all American families have the same amount of food?

Next, in the classroom, students create their own pretend supermarket, complete with name tags representing different foods, pricing, stations for students to be cashiers, and receipts. They thus gain first-hand experience as both shoppers and tellers, managers and distributors, and so on. This is followed by a spring activity where students harvest the school's own garden and consider scientific and environmental questions such as how insects can be beneficial. During the unit, they are introduced to new vocabulary words that reflect aspects of food production and distribution, such as *nutrients, manure, profit, display, cooler, bar-code, isles, cargo jets*, and *conveyor belt*.

Students also learn about the difference between solids and liquids; how the processes of freezing and melting, evaporating, crystallization, and condensing work scientifically. They experiment with using yeast to make bread and discuss what happens when you mix ingredients. Do the components change when mixed? Can we separate them again? They explore the mixing of different concrete materials, such as gravel (which doesn't change); pasta (which absorbs water but doesn't dissolve); and salt and sugar, which completely dissolve into the solution in which they are mixed.

These scientific activities are accompanied by readings such as *The Full Scoop*, about an African American inventor who created ways to store and transport ice cream. Students also take a variety of other field trips, such as to the Valley Sheppard Creamery and Howell Farms. Seeing food grown and harvested in different contexts helps students make important connections to what they are learning in language arts, math, science, and social studies. It requires students to learn the skills of close observation and research and combine them with experimentation and documentation.

In this unit of study, students embrace risk by exploring something integral to their everyday lives—food—in a broader and more critical context. As students come to understand that food impacts the entire world economy and ecology, they may rethink their own choices about how they procure food and what they eat at home.

EXAMPLE 2

MORE THAN JUST A BUILDING . . .

In seventh-grade American history and science classes, Wissahickon teachers set aside time each week for students to study a different part of the school building and relate it to the history of the Industrial Age. At one time, the school building was part of one of the largest radio factories in the world. Students thus begin by exploring the school building and making observations about how the space might have been used. For example, the upstairs has a vast open space where factory assembly lines operated.

Students also look at historic photos and examine them for scientific details that can help them understand the relationship between the design of the building and the conditions under which people worked. Students look at the sawtooth roof, and understand how it was designed to maximize efficiency of natural light when electricity was still new. When students go out in back of the building, they can see remnants of an old railroad and find historical artifacts.

After learning more about working in the Industrial Age, students relate this knowledge to what they know about work experience today, including interviews with people who currently work in the complex in which the school building is set. (There are twenty-five companies on the same piece of land as the school, all sharing the same address.) Students ask present-day workers to describe their typical workday and what they like about their jobs, and they collect artifacts from the person they interviewed.

This enables them to design a museum exhibit comparing one aspect of work in the Industrial Age to the present, using two artifacts (one historical and one contemporary) and writing historical and creative narratives. As part of this process, students go to historical museums to see how exhibits are designed.

As part of their work in the science classroom, students build a working radio from found objects (such as bottles and telephone handles). They explore the transfer of sound waves and energy and the science of the ear. This study of hard science is blended with issues of accessibility, politics, resources, and innovation.

Students explore the idea of "history empathy" and "multiple viewpoints." At the end of the unit, each student chooses a viewpoint (e.g., robber barons, women, children, African Americans) and examines events specifically from that perspective; they make podcasts of "I am" poems written from the perspective they chose. This is a risky assignment because it asks students to voice points of view that they may personally find objectionable. The value, however, is clear: students come to understand that whatever their viewpoint, learning about the past can help them play a more active role in shaping the future.

WISSAHICKON'S OUTDOOR PROGRAM

Children who grow up in cities, and particularly those who live in poor urban communities, often have little opportunity to play outside, and even less opportunity to explore and navigate natural settings like woods and mountains. The Wissahickon Charter School, in an urban area of the city of Philadelphia but with access to a nearby nature center and on-site garden, has created a unique curriculum that blends hands-on student exploration of both urban and rural environments.

This curriculum is supplemented by a variety of special trips designed to supplement the curriculum, raise critical questions about caring for the environment, and increase student confidence in completing challenging tasks—many of which require trust, collaboration, and courage. Through this process, students also come to see one another in different contexts—students who are not naturally academic leaders in the classroom, for example, may take on leadership roles on trips.

In addition to visiting local sites like the John Heinz National Wildlife Refuge, the Fairmount Water Works, the Schuylkill River, the Adventure Aquarium, and Island Beach State Park, students as young as fourth grade go on monthly hiking expeditions along with an occasional fishing trip. Fifth-graders go on overnight cabin camping trips, while sixth-graders camp in tents at a variety of sites across the East Coast. Once a year, fourth-, fifth- and sixth-graders go together on a five-day trip to a Vermont farm. By middle school, students are involved in backpacking expeditions, evolving into full-blown Outward Bound trips.

In all cases, students learn about outdoor survival skills (e.g., setting up tarps and tying knots, building fires, food preparation, dealing with wild animals). They also consider why it's important not to leave trash, and, more broadly, that how they leave the environment will ultimately impact others. Co-CEO Jamal Elliot says, "We have a stake in not merely teaching for today, but for tomorrow." Students also become active in the process of community building as they learn to support one another, and discover that each student has important and diverse skills to offer the group (for example, some can cook and others can be caregivers).

Students also come to see urban problems in a new light as they understand that cities are consciously constructed based on the attributes of the land. As with the Sustainable Cities project, they begin to ask questions about the positive and negative impacts of industrialization. Students keep journals throughout their travels. Central questions that they investigate on these trips include how to create communities that respect, value, and care for the land they are built on.

The trips also reinforce the belief that all valuable knowledge doesn't come from books. For example, students learn about the math and science of rotation while playing basketball or the impact of different angles while milking cows. Students also come to understand how to solve problems that are *immediate* in nature, when the consequences of ignoring them might seriously impact other students, such as helping each other across a ropes course or navigating a rocky path. Along the way, students also naturally come to appreciate what they have—even in impoverished neighborhoods—when those resources (such as electricity) are no longer easily available. As environmental educator Ann Pelo notes:

> In a culture that values intellect more than intuition or emotion, typical environmental education too often emphasizes facts and information in lieu of experience. . . . Our challenge is to see with new eyes, to look at the familiar as though we're seeing it for the first time.[1]

Interviews with students confirm that these trips are not only a favorite part of their experience at Wissahickon, but that they have a lasting impact on how students think about living their daily lives. Over and over, students talk about how their initial fear of trying something they deemed "risky" (climbing a mountain), "scary" (walking through the woods at night, avoiding wild bears), or downright "disgusting" (milking cows) was radically challenged by their engagement on these trips.

Students came back empowered by their own willingness to try to accomplish new things. As one student commented: "When we milked the cows, we had to taste the milk. I was surprised. It actually tasted good. It tasted like melted vanilla ice cream. It was warm. You get used to it." Another student recalled that when they first went on night hikes they were worried about something "popping out at them," a concern that soon relaxed into natural curiosity and enjoyment of the suspense of not knowing everything.

Students also returned with critical questions about what will happen to these natural spaces in years to come and a desire to brainstorm how they can have a positive impact. According to the school's co-CEOs:

> Many of our students haven't been outside the city of Philadelphia. These trips expand their knowledge of what is possible for them. . . . These trips are valuable, too, because they give students the chance to see nature that is less mediated by humans. We feel these trips help students see the importance of preserving natural spaces and it leaves them with a deeper commitment to creating a city that is sustainable that values the nature within it.

QUESTIONS TO CONSIDER:

- What does it mean to create a pedagogy where students "live the curriculum" and/or are involved in "purposeful investigation"? How is this the same as or different from what is more commonly known as "action research"? In your opinion, what are the *benefits* and *risks* of adopting this approach as a fundamental part of the school's mission?
- Based on the examples in this chapter, how would you reconstruct your current curriculum so that students have more opportunities to both identify and attempt to solve real-world problems, locally, nationally, or globally?
- What opportunities do students in your school have to *formally* learn outside the classroom? For example, does the school curriculum encompass critical questions and supervised activities that take place in the surrounding community and involve professionals within the community?
- Keeping in mind available resources, what opportunities exist in your school for students to help design the physical environment? This could be as simple as rearranging classroom furniture or helping choose the school lunch menu. In what ways do you think students benefit from these kinds of opportunities? How does it connect to the formal curriculum?
- If you had the resources and authority to supplement your curriculum with student trips (daily or overnight), what kinds of trips would you design? How, specifically, would it enrich your teaching about a particular topic or skill? What kinds of social or academic abilities would you want students to acquire as a result of their participation?
- Does your school have anything similar to Wissahickon's "Morning Meeting" (regardless of the time of day it occurs)? In other words, in what ways does your school attempt to create a community among students, staff, and

parents that is perceived as both safe and fun, and in which students have genuine opportunities to voice their opinions, concerns, ideas, and questions?

NOTES

1. Ann Pelo, "A Pedagogy for Equity," in *Rethinking Schools* 23, no. 4 (Summer 2009): 33.

2. Some of the teachers who worked collaboratively on developing the curricula in this chapter include: Jon Scherer, Michael Friedman, Merridy Gnagey and Jen Wong.

Chapter Six

Conclusion

It is time now to spell out and summarize the themes that run through this book, in the hope that you will find ways to use—or improve upon—them in your own work.

The ideas here are not new; many of them can be easily traced to the rich history of progressive education and can be found in the work of contemporary school visionaries and school case studies far too numerous to list (see the bibliography for a start). As you read this list, and consider the concrete examples of *embracing risk* drawn from the four schools profiled in this book, think about how you would revise it. What would you add? What do you disagree with? What are some of the positive or negative consequences of using such approaches? Do any elements of this list contradict or undermine one another?

Finally, ask yourself the most important question of all: What is your own definition of *embracing risk* in education?

PROJECT-BASED AND TRANSDISCIPLINARY LEARNING

This is a pedagogical approach to teaching and learning that encourages students to engage in complex, hands-on problem-solving activities and to think about alternative solutions to these problems as contexts change and new resources and information become available.

This kind of problem-solving is an inherently interdisciplinary, or more accurately *transdisciplinary* undertaking; rarely does a real-world problem require students to use math skills in isolation from science, history, or literacy. Indeed, the word *transdisciplinary* suggests that math, science, history, and other school subjects are not discrete activities, but are highly dependent on one another. For example, a store's cost for buying supplies from different vendors can be reduced in the classroom to a simple math equation. However, most store owners must consider the complex relationship between the cost of goods and whether to buy in bulk, expiration dates and storage space, the cost of labor (transportation, shelving, etc.), advertising and product preferences, environmental safety, and competition and community needs.

Project-based learning is often a multistage process that spans much more than a single class period and is not limited to a particular subject. Often it involves an essential question or question*s* that can frame an entire semester or year.

Finally, project-based learning, like many ways to *embrace risk* in education, requires ongoing input, reflection, and revision; students must be innovative and creative, working toward an endpoint that is rarely predetermined.

INQUIRY-BASED LEARNING

Inquiry-based learning is a pedagogical approach where students are encouraged to ask questions *at all points in the process*, including critical or skeptical questions, and questions that might challenge or change the direction of the lesson (for example, by providing an alternative point of view that reframes the premise or material on which the lesson is based).

Inquiry-based learning presupposes that teachers to do not hold all the answers and release them at prescribed intervals; instead, questions arise naturally and spontaneously from all members of the classroom community. Even assessments and tests (typically focused on definitive answers) can become question-oriented, as asking students to define what they do not understand or can't agree upon, or what still doesn't make sense, can be a complex and meaningful part of the learning process.

Finally, inquiry-based learning is premised on the idea that knowledge is never stagnant, that ideas and truths are always changing and contestable and need to be explored in specific contexts.

GIVING "SECOND CHANCES"

Along with the idea of "No Excuses," popular reform rhetoric often emphasizes the idea that there are no "second chances." The underlying message is that process is much less important than product, and schools must, like businesses, operate on the principal of efficiency and a bottom line. By contrast, embracing second chances requires that *reflection* and *revision* be an intrinsic part of all learning.

Moreover, reflection and revision must occur at multiple points in the learning process (not just at the end of an assignment), and be initiated both by teachers *and by students themselves*. This gives students opportunities to improve their process and ideas, look for new (sometimes conflicting) sources, rethink their initial assumptions and question their certainties, and recover from their so-called mistakes.

Embracing second chances means creating a safe environment based on trust and respect rather than carrots and sticks, and where "failure" is viewed as an important leg on the road to success and a fundamental part of learning. In this way, students also learn that equity and/or social change is a process of commitment, persistence, and renewal. In contrast, teaching students that there are no second chances encourages a kind of defeatism that leads them to believe that they are ultimately powerless to produce change if their first attempt is less than perfect.

LETTING STUDENTS WORK COLLABORATIVELY AND CONSIDER MULTIPLE POINTS OF VIEW

Although it can be harder to control and assess student achievement in this format, collaboration gives students a range of organizing and leadership skills—such as active listening, respectful critique, mediation and compromise, empathy, and respect for diversity and dissent.

It also reflects the kinds of situations students will encounter as they join the workforce, live in a technologically connected and globally interdependent polity, and negotiate issues of equity in the context of personal and public investments.

Moreover, when students work collaboratively, there is less likelihood that they will be given simplistic labels like "stupid" or "smart." One student may be good at solving math equations, while another might have a good eye for creative graphing and illustration, and another might be able to use the data in a compelling narrative "advertisement" for a product or to support a policy. Students bring different skills to the table.

DEPRIVATIZING TEACHING

The traditional classroom features a teacher working in relative isolation and as the ultimate authority, but this model is changing rapidly with the advent of collaborative teaching, interdisciplinary learning, mixed age-group classrooms, and teacher/action research.

Rather than pit teachers against one another as competitors (an ideology that is further enforced by proposals for merit pay based on standardized test scores, etc.) schools should encourage teachers to learn from one another's practice and jointly develop ideas that will enrich all teaching and learning.

Opportunities for teachers of different disciplines to jointly create project-based activities for groups of students, or to follow a theme or question across a number of classes, also enrich learning for students and help teachers to stimulate real-world learning and to be more creative in their work. For example, the science teacher might have students write biographies of scientists in conjunction with the English teacher, and then work with the visual arts/technology teacher to make them into videos.

In fact, students can play a large role in this process. Ideally, knowledge should flow in all directions, as students themselves have experiences, sources of information, opinions, and ideas that can be fundamental to the learning process. Students should have opportunities to formally present/ share their ideas, and to respectfully critique one another's work.

RELEVANCE IS NEVER IRRELEVANT

To be meaningful to students, learning should build both on their prior experiences and knowledge, and on their unexplored questions and internal curiosity. Students thus must see what they are doing in school as relevant, significant and stimulating; this is what Jacqueline Ancess calls a "need to know" atmosphere.[1] In other words, students are much more likely to retain information that they can find applications for or that they feel will help them make important decisions they face daily.

As many concrete examples in this book underscore, however, this does not mean rejecting the study of classic history and literature texts, or teaching about cultures not represented in the classroom. Rather, it means using them creatively to raise broader, essential questions, to make connections between history and current events, and to let students apply and reinterpret what they've learned in new contexts.

Ideally, this should include the opportunity use current technologies, and to draw on a wide range of forms of personal expression, such as the arts and folk arts, community speeches, teach-ins, writing letters to newspapers and politicians, collecting oral histories, and conducting research on community needs and popular opinion.

FOSTERING "COURAGEOUS CONVERSATIONS"

As in society itself, in every school there are issues that are difficult to talk openly about. These include potentially uncomfortable or contentious issues like racism, sexism, religion, poverty, and homophobia. When schools do not provide forums for students to discuss these issues, they don't disappear or cease to be relevant.

Such opportunities must be built into the school's mission and structure, curriculum and professional development, rather than be viewed as something that happens spontaneously and is peripheral to the central purpose of education. They should not, in other words, be relegated to special assemblies, holidays, or specific times like Black History Month.

Moreover, in the case of something like bullying, schools should not limit themselves to distributing mandates and behavioral worksheets without opportunities for discussion and analysis. Both students and teachers must have safe, guided, *ongoing* opportunities to talk about these issues in various groupings and contexts—both within the formal classroom and in other school spaces. And whoever is helping to create and guide these conversations should be conscious of the fact that silences can be very meaningful and can stem from different psychological roots (fear, intimidation, willful resistance, ignorance, self-protection, etc.).

OUTSIDE/IN CLASSROOMS

Although they often try to function as such, schools do not exist in isolation. They are part of larger communities, cultures, and social systems, and the more opportunities students have to explore and engage in those communities, the more likely it is they will become advocates and change agents. As much as possible, then, what goes on in the classroom should be tied to opportunities for volunteer and in-service work connected to real-world problem-solving and support.

Likewise, there should be diverse opportunities for family and community members—artists, elders, historians, and other adults who have experience and wisdom to share—to come into the classroom and interact with students in a genuine and sustained manner.

MULTITASKING

Many conservative educators seek to measure student time "on-task," as evidenced by external factors such as silence, eye contact, and answering questions when prompted. There is nothing wrong with wanting students to be focused and mindful about learning. But the larger goal should not be to pile information on top of information for the purpose of recall without analysis.

In other words, it's not just important to assess what we know and how we know things to be true, but also what we don't know or don't agree on. Students need to investigate the mechanisms through which knowledge is validated, disciplined, silenced, generated, and reconstructed. As Dewey suggests, one of our greatest pedagogical fallacies is the belief that students only learn one thing at a time.

KNOWLEDGE IS NOT A COMMODITY OR A PRIZE

We cannot, in other words, be "out-educated" by other countries, or other school systems. Critical thinking, inquiry, investigation, and analysis are not things that can be lost to others or taken away. When we talk about being "out-educated," then, the underlying discussion is not about knowledge, but about power and control and cultural supremacy.

Rather than seeing the educational growth of other countries as threatening or demeaning, we need to create a global curriculum, considering how certain issues and problems impact the entire planet (albeit in different ways), and promoting the ethic of collaboration and resource sharing.

Moreover, motivation to learn should be nurtured from within the student rather than as something external and material. When we equate learning solely with getting good grades, test scores, and awards, we send the message to students that what they are doing is not intrinsically worthy of investigation, and further, that they can only succeed at the expense of others.

OPENING THE CLASSROOM DOOR

Though many schools are designed to structure and organize every moment of the students' day—including how they walk down the halls or with whom they eat lunch—students continue to find ways to interact and relate to each other in ways that are not socially sanctioned. Put another way, whether we acknowledge it or not, learning takes place in the hallways, lunchrooms, gyms, schoolyards, playgrounds, and school gardens, as well as on class trips, school fundraisers, celebrations, parent events, and exchange programs.

Schools are enriched by opportunities for students to interact with and think critically about their relationships with others in different contexts. Moreover, students should be able to see themselves as more than just an academic label ("at-risk" or "proficient") at the cost of marginalizing or ignoring other important skills, intelligences, qualities, and leadership skills that cannot be adequately demonstrated in the classroom alone.

RESPECTING DISSENT INSTEAD OF PUNISHING IT (OR "CREATIVE MALADJUSTMENT")

Ancess has written prolifically about creating school environments where "student resistance and ambivalence, often regarded as pathological willfulness, is normalized."[2] Sam Chaltain calls this process learning and contribution "through freedom not conformity."[3] Schools that *embrace risk* want to hear what their students have to say, creating varied opportunities for *school-wide* examination, exploration, and critique.

This is not the same as tolerating rudeness or destructiveness. Obviously, students must learn how to voice their opinions in constructive ways—a process that can often be modeled for them by teachers and administrators who do the same. Kohl suggests that when children rebel against poverty and prejudice and refuse to conform and take their "proper place" in the hierarchy of power and privilege, they are "maladjusting." Kohl believes that "it is their teachers' place to make that maladjustment functional and creative rather than to suppress it."[4]

In addition to being able to critique the obvious, students must have opportunities to explore what is often called the *hidden curriculum*, meaning assumptions and ideologies that are not explicitly stated, but are very much embedded in what students are learning. Finally, students should have the freedom to make salient distinctions between "excuses" (often assumed to be personal in nature) and larger systemic analysis and explanations.

EXPLORING INTERSECTIONALITY

Of course we want to be sensitive to cultural differences. But we must appreciate the complexity and subjectivity of these identities. Instead of talking about "immigrants" as if they were all the same, for example, teachers should recognize that people immigrate for many different reasons and under many different conditions.

Likewise, the experience of being black may be very different depending upon the color of one's skin, as well as important factors like gender and class. Ideological constructions such as "The Welfare Queen," for example, depend upon the intersection of race, class, and gender.

Schools, then, must help students to refuse to accept surface cultural stereotyping, generalizations, and other simplistic explanations for why people make the choices they make. Students should always be guided to dig deeper, ask more critical questions, and consider that in every cultural/historical group there are significant differences in power and privilege, and, moreover, that these differences are shifting, interacting, and contestable.

Also, schools should seek to understand and explore cultural differences in real-world contexts, rather than erase them, ignore them, or try to see past them.

REJECTING DEFICIT MODELS OF TEACHING AND LEARNING

Many schools, especially those comprising large numbers of children considered "at-risk," operate under the assumption that their job is to "save" students and "intervene." This often means that students' home cultures, communities, and first languages are seen solely as barriers that must be overcome and replaced by a common "American" ethos. A deficit approach to teaching and learning also assumes that students are essentially "products" to be ranked, sorted, improved (or, if absolutely necessary, *discontinued*) by their potential "value-added."

Schools, then, must challenge the assumption that the time underprivileged children spend outside the school building (in their own cultures and communities) is necessarily "wasted" time, or has no educational value. This also means that a longer school day does not necessarily create deeper and more sustained student learning and commitment to school. In fact, it may increase alienation and frustration.

EXPLORING EMPATHY AND EXPERIENTIAL LEARNING

In addition to more traditional in-service and community-enrichment activities, there are many ways that teachers can bridge theory with practice. Teachers, for example, should consider pedagogical approaches that ask students to think about how intellectual concepts like "oppression" or "colonialism" *feel*.

This might mean asking students to use different parts of their bodies other than just their brains by engaging in simulations, interpretive movement, or symbolic representation. Moreover, while many schools ask students to keep journals or write biographical essays or memoirs, it is also important that students have the opportunity to tell *someone else's story*.

Finally, schools should consider opportunities for students to travel or live in a radically different environment/culture (ranging from camping trips to exchange programs) as a way of coming to see things they may take for granted in a new light.

LITERACY REQUIRES NAVIGATION SKILL

In the twenty-first century, youth are used to what might be called "information overload." New technologies allow them to access information instantly, and to engage in real-time conversations with others near and far away. The classroom, in other words, has greatly expanded, and the textbook is becoming a thing of the past. This makes it more important than ever that students evaluate the *credibility* of sources (including websites and photographs). Students need to learn how to use technology thoughtfully and effectively. Finally, the concept of "literacy" must expand to include a wide range of multimedia. Students must develop a critical literacy that gives them the skills to sift through and combine seemingly endless and often conflicting information to dispute, validate, and/or create new knowledge.

DEALING WITH DISRUPTION

In *The Global Achievement Gap*, Tony Wagner reminds us that traditional schools are primarily concerned with rewarding students who get *the right answer*. Yet, as Wagner rightly notes: "To be comfortable with this new economy and environment, you have to understand that you live in a world where there isn't one right answer, or if there is, it's right only for a nanosecond. If you're afraid, you can't think clearly."[5]

From the events of 9/11 to the Great Recession, to recent regime changes in foreign countries, to shifts in political power in the United States government, to a hurricane in New Orleans and a tsunami in Japan, future leaders must be able to deal with unexpected and exogenous factors and "disruptions"—both locally and globally.

This means, as Wagner suggests, that students should be prepared for disruption rather than constantly fearing it. Although some situations have no clear positive value, students should still be able to see disruption as an opportunity to act with courage and vision.

ASSESSMENT THAT REWARDS RISK

This is last on the list, because in many ways it is the most obvious. Schools that *embrace risk* must also reward it. In other words, teachers and students can't be encouraged to engage in debate and critical inquiry if they are only going to be tested in narrow, multiple-choice formats.

Likewise, rather than worrying about "wrong answers" and "bad ideas," students should be *rewarded* for experimenting and taking chances, for asking new questions, and for persisting in seeking better solutions or redefining the problems themselves. This means that we cannot embrace risk without radically rethinking concepts of assessment and accountability. Curiosity, creativity, and courage—along with persistence, commitment, and sustained innovation—should be weighed heavily in the assessment and grading process.

In contrast to high-stakes, once-a-year tests, assessment that embraces and rewards risk:

- is a multifaceted process that takes place throughout the lesson plan;
- is tied to student inquiry and reflection, not just memorization and recall;
- requires students to demonstrate an understanding of the relationship between *theory* and *practice*, that is, how knowledge is *framed* and *used* in different contexts and for different political and ideological purposes;
- emphasizes the importance of learning skills within an *interdisciplinary* or *transdisciplinary* framework (as real-world problem-solving almost always requires);
- gives students opportunities to contribute to and respectfully critique each other's work (and in some cases to design the tests themselves); and

- allows students to present their work to an audience, stakeholder group, "expert," and/or "authority" beyond their own teachers—such as larger groups of students (at their own and other schools), community groups, policy makers, and cultural leaders who can engage with students in meaningful discuss and debate.

I have tried to underscore that in schools that *embrace risk* as part of the assessment process, students must still work hard and take personal responsibility; concretely demonstrate mastery and achievement; and explore and understand a wide range of facts and skills, including reading "classic" texts, doing high-level math, and mastering complex scientific theories.

A main premise of this book has been to contest the idea that if we don't standardize the curriculum and embrace a culture of "teaching to the test," students will not learn anything *concrete*, *measurable*, or *quantifiable*. The examples in this book demonstrate that in addition to the qualities above, we must also seek to assess whether student learning will likely be sustained, meaningful, critical, and adaptable. At times, this may mean trying to assess learning when it is "unfinished," meaning that students do not have to demonstrate that they "know it all," only that they have the skills to continue engaging, learning, creating, reflecting, and reimagining.

I end this book, then, with questions for educators, test designers and policymakers to consider when creating assessments that *embrace risk*:

- Is the student asked to consider multiple perspectives, sources, or versions of "the truth"? If so, does the student demonstrate critical analysis regarding the origin and/or impact of such differences?
- Can the student demonstrate different forms of analysis, and ask critical questions about their interaction? For example, combining discourse analysis *and* media literacy?
- Likewise, if something is not in the student's native language, or is from a cultural perspective the student has no knowledge of, does the student have the skills to proceed investigating without resorting to stereotypes or easy assumptions?
- Is there an opportunity for the student to ask his or her own questions, and/or to point out incongruences and contradictions in assessment process?
- Can the student make connections between decontextualized content (e.g., facts) and contemporary real-world problems? Likewise, is the student able to consider (imagine) the relevance of knowledge in changing contexts?
- Is the student able to consider how knowledge from other disciplines might change or enhance their understanding of a particular disciplinary question?

- Is the student given opportunities for "second chances," meaning: (a) multiple opportunities for assessment throughout project/lesson/assignment; (b) multiple opportunities to reflect on work; (c) multiple opportunities after project has ended to consider what they would do differently next time, or another line of related questions they would like to pursue?
- Does the student demonstrate the qualities of curiosity, healthy skepticism, and open-mindedness?
- In addition to showing their mastery of content knowledge, does the student create new knowledge and/or utilize their imagination to consider alternatives?
- Does the student demonstrate an ability to work collaboratively and productively with other students, especially students they either don't know well or whose opinions they do not necessarily agree with?
- When conflict arises is the student able to comfortably voice their opinion and respectfully argue their point of view?
- Likewise, when working in a group is the student able to demonstrate different kinds of leadership roles? Is the student able to demonstrate skills involved in effective leadership, including: *active listening*, *synthesizing of ideas*, *mediation*, *critique*, and *delineating responsibilities (in both a top-down and bottom-up process depending upon the circumstances)?*
- Can the student deconstruct how certain questions are "framed" and the role of different stakeholders and politics in the framing process? Can the student identify the "hidden curriculum," often describing those questions, experiences, ideologies, or facts that are *not* visible or open to question?
- Is the student asks to demonstrate how a particular concept (e.g., racism) *feels?* Can students make connections among different kinds of inequity and injustice, without oversimplifying culture? In other words, has the student demonstrated an understanding of the significance of *intersectionality*?
- Is the student asked to engage in (age-appropriate) research and analysis, such as action/participatory research, ethnography, written surveys, or oral interviews? Can students distinguish between different methodologies and can they make informed choices about how to decide between them or blend them? Are they able to consider the pros and cons of different approaches, and to engage in triangulation of data?
- Does student assessment utilize the vast range of available technologies? Likewise, does assessment allow students to express what they have learned in a variety of oral, written, musical, and visual mediums?
- Does student assessment recognize that actions can often speak as loudly as words (e.g., volunteering in a shelter or organizing a fundraiser for the homeless maybe equally as valuable or more valuable than knowing statistics about the homeless)?

- When the student is asked to engage in in-service learning, does their reflection demonstrate that they are learning as much as they are "giving," and, further, that their preconceived ideas are being challenged? Is reflection an ongoing and critical part of the in-service experience?
- Does the assessment require students to answer a question similar to that posed by SLA principal Chris Lehmann: *"What is the worst consequence of your best idea?"* In other words, when exploring the unknown, are students asked to assess the risks while simultaneously encouraged to embrace them?

NOTES

1. Jacqueline Ancess, *Beating the Odds: High Schools as Communities of Commitment* (New York: Teachers College Press, 2003).

2. Ancess, *Beating the Odds*, 128.

3. Sam Chaltain, *American Schools: The Art of Creating a Democratic Learning Community* (Lanham, MD: Rowman & Littlefield, 2010), 63.

4. Herbert Kohl, *"I Won't Learn from You"—and Other Thoughts on Creative Maladjustment* (New York: The New Press, 1994), 152.

5. Tony Wagner, *The Global Achievement Gap* (New York: Basic Books, 2008), 31–32.

Appendix

Contemporary Educators Respond: "How Would You Define Embracing Risk in Urban Education?"

"Of course we put our children at risk by imposing 'a crust of conventionality' by withholding space and opportunity sufficient to free them to speak and think for themselves as participant members and shapers of the 'community in the making' John Dewey saw as democracy. At once, by depriving them of opportunities to imagine what might be and to act on what they feel to be their possibilities, their elders or authorizes prevent them from taking the transformative risks of growing, of becoming different—of humanization."

—Dr. Maxine Greene, professor of education, Teachers College, Columbia, and director of the Foundation for the Social Imagination, the Arts and Education

"I think we need to reframe our thinking of what it means to be 'at-risk,' because, as I saw it, my students were also always 'at-risk' of something great, 'at-risk' of letting their intellect, passion, artistry, cultural and political awareness, humor, and youthful wisdom shine through. They were constantly 'at-risk' of educational success, even as they confronted and fought off the twin demons of self-doubt and low skills. Being 'at-risk' didn't just bind my students to their conditions, it also pointed toward their potential to transform their own lives."

—Dr. Wayne Au, assistant professor, University of Washington, and editor of *Rethinking Schools*

"The pejorative connotation of 'at-risk,' especially when attached to the name of an urban teen of color, often occludes the strengths, capacities, and life-affirming energy of the young person—their creativity and myriad possibilities. . . . Perhaps were we to focus on the 'funds of knowledge' found in their communities, we might see these young people differently, not as 'damaged goods' who are 'at-risk' of all sorts of dead-ends, but as 'persons in the making' who shouldn't be reduced to a label that represents our judgment about their destiny. "

—Dr. Margaret Smith Crocco, dean of the College of Education at the University of Iowa

"Embracing risk in education moves us to question our foundations of 'knowing,' it reveals the processes in place which connect students to their developing understanding and awareness of subject matter, and it also reveals what is left unsaid and unclaimed in the very field of knowledge production. . . . To me, embracing risk is constitutive of the learning process. Without risks, we find ourselves at a stalemate. . . . I do think we need change in our schools, but I think it stems from below, from an active engagement with our surroundings, with history and with each other. It means taking risks that are purposeful and deliberate."

—Dr. Nathalia Jaraqmillo, professor of Education, Purdue University

"Both teaching and learning involve risk. The risk to be vulnerable and to not know. The risk to step outside of what is familiar to embrace change and uncertainty. It suggests risking failure and disappointment. To embrace risk requires a climate of trust. Currently in the US, and especially in urban districts, rather than trust there is often a climate of mistrusting teachers, which has led to substituting the reading of scripts and high stakes testing for authentic teaching. If we trust teachers to take risks, we give them the knowledge and support to create classrooms where there is a lively exchange of ideas and students and teachers risk not knowing and take on the struggle to learn. If we trust students, then we allow them to explore outside of the boundaries of our and their knowledge; we allow them to take the risk of not knowing in order to know and to learn."

—Dr. Katherine Schultz, dean, School of Education, Mills College

"Students are developing their sense of power and agency at a very precarious time, at a constituent moment during a world historical epidemic of capitalist overproduction. . . . and where *at-risk* students have been consigned to the rag-and-bone shop of expendability. . . . If young people are to survive this crisis, they need to understand it, and develop the skills to fight it, and to transform it. . . . (Yet) we can never create a pedagogy with faultless legitimacy, one that never contradicts the basic principles which directed them from the beginning. . . . Critical pedagogy neither guarantees political upheaval nor stable states of social brotherhood and sisterhood. . . . If we believe that theory is universally fixed then we will not be making history, rather, history will be making us."

— Dr. Peter McLaren, professor in the Division of Urban Schooling, Graduate School of Education and Information, University of California, Los Angeles

"I find it difficult to think about risk, or the taking of risks, without simultaneously thinking about hope—and fear. Choice also comes to mind. . . . Hope is a function and reflection of the human capacity to create and make choices, to not only be made by history, but to also make history. To hope, and to be human, in this regard, entails risk and the taking of risks, and the taking—and sharing—of responsibility for choices made. This is because when one takes risks, one also sets into motion new risks for others. . . . Some of us can, with impunity, take risks, while others experience risk as a consequence of others' choices. . . . This, disturbingly, has been the prevailing life for poor kids and poor, urban kids of color for quite some time. . . . We collectively risk not only the remaining shards of our democracy but also the possibility of our humanity if we continue to deny urban kids the right and opportunities to choose, to take risks, to hope—to be human."

— Dr. Christopher Robbins, associate professor of social foundations, Department of Teacher Education, Eastern Michigan University

"The most important thing we can do as educators is to provide [at-risk] youngsters with experiences that will create in them the sense of agency, entitlement, and confidence that is so abundant in their affluent counterparts and that enables them to be successful."

— Dr. Jacqueline Ancess, co-director, National Center for Restructuring Education, Schools and Teaching (NCREST), and professor of education, Teachers College, Columbia University

"The risk many students face in maintaining their cultural practices, not that their culture itself should be labeled 'at-risk.' I often wonder is it worse to be invisible or commoditized—or misappropriated, or appropriated? . . . We must ask: 'Was the risk we took effective? Who is taking the real risk?' We must support risk without supporting the *glamorization* of risk and the tools of protest."

— Deborah Wei, former director of Asian Americans United and founding principal of FACTS

"We need to change the terms used in educational policy discourse. 'School readiness' is a school problem, not a child problem. I never saw a child come to kindergarten who was not 'ready to learn;' I have seen lots of early grades classrooms that were not ready to teach children in the ways they needed to be taught—*to risk* engaging the children's knowledge and interests, teaching in culturally responsive ways, providing a proper mix of support and challenge."

—Dr. Frederick Erickson, professor of anthropology of education, Graduate School of Education and Information Studies, University of California, Los Angeles, and past director and founder of the Center for Urban Ethnography

"Risk is part and parcel of teaching and learning. Sadly, as a society we are much more willing to allow children of means and their teachers to risk, fail, learn from the experience, and try again than we are of students who attend schools for 'at-risk' kids where a single year of 'failure' or less than adequate progress on high stakes standardized tests results in dire consequences. Opportunities to take the risks required for all children to learn and grow must be paired with patience, perseverance and trust. The irony, of course is that those students labeled 'at-risk,' are the very ones who learn in environments where the risks required for learning to occur and the trust necessary to learn from 'failure' are in the shortest supply."

—Dr. Erin Horvat, associate professor of urban education, Temple University

"It was early in my special education career that I read about children with different risk profiles. What if, as educators, we change our perceptions and language to include children with different *success* profiles? How much more positive the teaching experience may be for both the student and teacher when we focus on students' strengths and abilities."

—Dr. Audrey Cohan, professor of education, Molloy College

"When students are identified as 'at-risk' we think of their schooling as a way to ameliorate this risk. But the protection afforded to children through schools is often misplaced—it focuses on the classroom rather than the school—and is therefore rendered ineffective. While the classroom is often overprotected—classrooms should be 'safe places,' we hear, where children can peacefully explore ideas, often at the expense of intellectual risk-taking—schools sometimes create or exacerbate many of the risks that children and youth face. These risks, including neglect, lack of opportunity, and despair, are the ones educators and administrators should tackle, and they require a brave look at the system as a whole, one that will allow schools to provide all children with pathways to greater opportunity."

—Dr. Sigal Ben-Porath, associate professor, Graduate School of Education, University of Pennsylvania

"For all of us, the most powerful learning experiences are the ones that push us outside of our comfort zones, and challenge us in ways that create the possibility that we might discover something new about ourselves, each other, and the larger world. Meaningful learning is risky, difficult, and sometimes painful. But it's also sometimes the moment when we first discover what we're capable of, and why we can never go back to the way we were."

—Dr. Sam Chaltain, former director of the Forum for Education and Democracy and founding director of the Five Freedoms Project

Selected Bibliography

Allender, J., and Sclarow Allender, D. (2008). *The Humanistic Teacher: First the Child and Then the Curriculum*. St. Paul, MN: Paradigm.

Ancess, J. (2003). *Beating the Odds: High Schools as Communities of Commitment*. New York: Teachers College Press.

Apple, M. (1993). *Official Knowledge: Democratic Education in a Conservative Age*. New York: Routledge.

Au, W. (2009). *Rethinking Multicultural Education: Teaching for Racial and Cultural Justice*. Milwaukee, WI: Rethinking Schools.

Bastian, A., Fruchter, N., Gittell, M., Greer, C., and Haskins, K. (1986). *Choosing Equity: The Case for Democratic Schooling*. Philadelphia: Temple University Press.

Ben-Porath, S. (2006). *Citizenship under Fire: Democratic Education in Times of Conflict*. Princeton, NJ: Princeton University Press.

Calabrese Barton, A. (2003). *Teaching Science for Social Justice*. New York: Teachers College Press.

Chaltain, S. (2010). *American Schools: The Art of Creating a Democratic Learning Community*. Lanham, MD: Rowman & Littlefield.

Collins, P. H. (2010). *Another Kind of Public Education: Race, Schools, the Media and Democratic Possibilities*. Boston: Beacon.

Cuban, L. (2004). *The Blackboard and the Bottom Line: Why Schools Can't Be Businesses*. Cambridge, MA: Harvard University Press.

Cuban, L., and Usdan, M. (2003). *Powerful Reforms with Shallow Roots: Improving America's Urban Schools*. New York: Teachers College Press.

Darling-Hammond, L. (2010). *The Flat World and Education: How America's Commitment to Equity Will Determine the Future*. New York: Teachers College Press.

———. (1997). *The Right to Learn: A Blueprint for Creating Schools That Work*. San Francisco: Jossey-Bass.

Darling-Hammond, L., French, J., and Garcia-Lopez, S. P. (2002). *Learning to Teach for Social Justice*. New York: Teachers College Press.

Delpit, L. (1995). *Other People's Children: Cultural Conflict in the Classroom*. New York: The New Press.

Dewy, J. (2005). *Democracy and Education*. New York: Barnes and Noble.

———. (1997). *Experience and Education*. New York: Free Press.

Duncan-Arcade, J., and Morrell, E. (2008). *The Art of Critical Pedagogy: Possibilities for Moving from Theory to Practice in Urban Schools*. New York: Peter Lang.

Evans-Winters, V. (2011). *Teaching Black Girls: Resiliency in Urban Classrooms*. New York: Peter Lang.

Fine, M. (1994). *Chartering Urban School Reform: Reflections on High Schools in the Midst of Change*. New York: Teachers College Press.

Fine, M., and Weis, L. (1993). *Beyond Silenced Voices: Class, Race, and Gender in United States Schools*. Albany: SUNY Press.

Finn, P. (1999). *Literacy with an Attitude: Educating Working-Class Children in Their Own Best Interests*. Albany: SUNY Press.

Freire, P. (1998). *Pedagogy of Freedom: Ethics, Democracy, and Civic Courage*. Lanham, MD: Rowman & Littlefield.

———. (2000). *Pedagogy of the Oppressed*. New York: Continuum.

Ginsberg, A.E., Shapiro, J.P. and Brown, S. (2004) Gender in Urban Education: Strategies for Student Achievement. Portsmouth, NH: Heinemann.

Giroux, H. (2001). *Theory and Resistance in Education*. Santa Barbara, CA: Praeger.

Goodland, J. (1994). *Educational Renewal: Better Teachers, Better Schools*. San Francisco: Jossey-Bass.

Goodman, K., Shannon, P., Goodman, Y., and Rapoport, R. (2004). *Saving Our Schools: The Case for Public Education Saying No to "No Child Left Behind."* Berkeley, CA: RDR Books.

Greene, M. (1988). *The Dialectic of Freedom*. New York: Teachers College Press.

———. (1995). *Releasing the Imagination: Essays on Education, the Arts, and Social Change*. San Francisco: Jossey-Bass.

Honigsfeld, A., and Cohan, A. (2010). *Breaking the Mold of School Instruction and Organization: Innovative and Successful Practices for the Twenty-First Century*. Lanham, MD: Rowman & Littlefield.

hooks, b. (1994). *Teaching to Transgress: Education as the Practice of Freedom*. New York: Routledge.

Johnson, L., Finn, M., and Lewis, R. (2005). *Urban Education with an Attitude*. Albany: SUNY Press.

Kogan, B. (1997). *Common Schools, Uncommon Futures: A Working Consensus for School Renewal*. New York: Teachers College Press.

Kohl, H. (1994). *"I Won't Learn from You"—and Other Thoughts on Creative Maladjustment*. New York: The New Press.

Kohn, A. (2011). *Feel-Bad Education: And Other Contrarian Essays on Children and Schooling*. Boston: Beacon.

———. (1999). *The Schools Our Children Deserve: Moving Beyond Traditional Classrooms and "Tougher Standards."* New York: Houghton Mifflin.

———. (2009). "When '21st-Century Schooling' Just Isn't Good Enough: A Modest Proposal." *Rethinking Schools* 23, no. 3 (Spring).

Kozal, J. (1991). *Savage Inequalities: Children in America's Schools*. New York: Crown.

Lytle, J. (2010). *Working for Kids: Leadership as Inquiry and Invention*. Lanham, MD: Rowman & Littlefield.

Lytle, S., and Cochran-Smith, M. (1992). *Inside/Outside: Teacher Research and Knowledge*. New York: Teachers College Press.

McLaren, P., and Sleeter, C. (1995). *Multicultural Education, Critical Pedagogy, and the Politics of Difference*. Albany, NY: SUNY.

Meirer, D., Kohn, A. Darling-Hammond, L., Sizer, T., and Wood, G. (2004). *Many Children Left Behind: How the No Child Left Behind Act Is Damaging Our Children and Our Schools*. Boston: Beacon.

Michie, G. (1999). *Holler If You Hear Me: The Education of a Teacher and His Students*. New York: Teachers College Press.

Nathan, L. (2009). *The Hardest Questions Aren't on the Test: Lessons from an Innovative Urban School*. Boston: Beacon.

Noguera, P. (2003). *City Schools and the American Dream: Reclaiming the Promise of American Education*. New York: Teachers College Press.

———. (2008). *The Trouble with Black Boys and Other Reflections on Race, Equity, and the Future of Public Education*. San Francisco: Jossey-Bass.

Ooka Pang, V. (1998). *Struggling to Be Heard: The Unmet Needs of Asian Pacific American Children*. Albany: SUNY Press.

Pelo, A. (2009). "A Pedagogy for Equity." *Rethinking Schools* 23, no. 4 (Summer).

Pollock, M. (2008). *Everyday Anti-Racism: Getting Real about Race in School*. New York: The New Press.

Postman, N., and Weingartner, C. (1969). *Teaching as a Subversive Activity*. New York: Delacorte.

Ravitch, D. (2010). *The Death and Life of the Great American School System: How Tests and Choice Are Undermining Education*. New York: Basic.

Robbins, C. (2008). *Expelling Hope: The Assault on Youth and the Militarization of Schooling*. Albany, NY: SUNY.

Rose, M. (1989). *Lives on the Boundary*. London: Penguin.

Sarason, S. (1996). *Revisiting "The Culture of the School and the Problem of Change."* New York: Teachers College Press.

Shapiro, J., and Stefkovich, J. (2010). *Ethical Leadership and Decision Making in Education: Applying Theoretical Perspectives to Complex Dilemmas*. New York: Routledge.

Shultz, J., and Cook-Sather, A. (2001). *In Our Own Words: Students' Perspectives on School*. Lanham, MD: Rowman & Littlefield.

Shultz, K. (2009). *Rethinking Classroom Participation: Listening to Silent Voices*. New York: Teachers College Press.

Thernstrom, A., and Thernstrom, S. (2003). *No Excuses: Closing the Racial Gap in Learning*. New York: Simon and Schuster.

Tyack, D., and Cuban, L. (1995). *Tinkering Toward Utopia: A Century of Public School Reform*. Cambridge, MA: Harvard University Press.

Wagner, T. (2008). *The Global Achievement Gap*. New York: Basic.

Weber, K. (2010). *Waiting for Superman: How We Can Save America's Schools*. New York: Public Affairs.

Woyshner, C., Wafrus, J., and Smith Crocco, M. (2004). *Social Education in the Twentieth Century*. New York: Peter Lang.

Index

About the Author

Dr. Alice E. Ginsberg researches and writes about urban education, critical pedagogy, educational equity and public policy. She is the author or editor of *Gender in Urban Education* (Heinemann, 2003), *Gender and Educational Philanthropy* (Palgrave, 2007), *The Evolution of American Women's Studies* (Palgrave, 2008), *And Finally We Meet: Feminist Activists, Academics and Students* (ITROW, 2011), and *Difficult Dialogues about 21st Century Girls* (forthcoming SUNY 2012).